ISBN 978-1-333-39766-1
PIBN 10499475

1 MONTH OF
FREE
READING

at
www.ForgottenBooks.com

By purchasing this book you are eligible for one month membership to ForgottenBooks.com, giving you unlimited access to our entire collection of over 700,000 titles via our web site and mobile apps.

To claim your free month visit:
www.forgottenbooks.com/free499475

English
Français
Deutsche
Italiano
Español
Português

www.forgottenbooks.com

Mythology Photography **Fiction**
Fishing Christianity **Art** Cooking
Essays Buddhism Freemasonry
Medicine **Biology** Music **Ancient**
Egypt Evolution Carpentry Physics
Dance Geology **Mathematics** Fitness
Shakespeare **Folklore** Yoga Marketing
Confidence Immortality Biographies
Poetry **Psychology** Witchcraft
Electronics Chemistry History **Law**
Accounting **Philosophy** Anthropology
Alchemy Drama Quantum Mechanics
Atheism Sexual Health **Ancient History**
Entrepreneurship Languages Sport
Paleontology Needlework Islam
Metaphysics Investment Archaeology
Parenting Statistics Criminology
Motivational

AN ATTEMPT

AT A

BIBLIOGRAPHY OF CYPRUS

BY

CLAUDE DELAVAL COBHAM

B.C.L. M.A. OXON. M.R.A.S.

COMMISSIONER OF LARNACA

FOURTH EDITION

NICOSIA

1900

65339435 ✓

Cat for ~~Ref~~ + Bib

D c coll

Pur

NOTE.

I HAVE attempted to register in these pages the titles of all books treating of Cyprus, its people, history, numismatics, epigraphy and language, of which I have found any trace. I have included the papers most important to antiquaries and linguists which have appeared in Magazines or in the Transactions of learned Societies ; also the few books printed in the Island between 1880 and 1887. I have added lists of local newspapers, of Maps, of Consular Reports and Parliamentary Papers, and of the fugitive pieces which record a controversy, not yet extinguished, concerning the " transformations and migrations" of Cypriot antiquities purchased from Signor L. P. di Cesnola by the Metropolitan Museum of Art at New York.

The " Book Law," No. II. of 1887, has been in force in the Island since July 1, 1887, and lists of books which have issued since that date from Cypriot presses may be found in the Cyprus Gazettes, Nos. 304, 334, 361, 398, 429, 464, 511, 538, 582, 618 and 658. I could have added largely to the bulk, but probably little to the value, of the list by including more of the ephemeral articles which will readily be found in the Indexes to Periodical Literature by Poole, Griswold, Miliaraki (Νεολληνικὴ γεωγραφικὴ φιλολογία, 8vo., Athens, 1889) and others. Herein a paper by Prof. Dr. Eugen Oberhummer (reprinted in 1893 by S. Calvary, at Berlin, from the Jahresbericht über die Fortschritte der Klassischen Altertumswissenschaft," Band 77) entitled " Bericht über Geographie von Griechenland, III. Teil, KYPROS," will be the student's best guide.

When the list was first circulated in June, 1886, it contained 152 titles. The edition of 1889 contained 309; that of 1894 497, and new sections of Cartography and Consular Reports. The present shows 728.

I have done, I think all I can for this little compilation. I reserve no rights in it, and shall be glad to see it corrected, extended and improved in any country by any Society or scholar interested in the subject. It were a counsel of perfection to suggest that the first section might be divided and re-arranged according to the subject matter of the books enumerated.

Larnaca,
    April 19, 1900.

AN ATTEMPT AT A BIBLIOGRAPHY OF CYPRUS.

SUCHEN, LUDOLFUS DE De Terra Sancta et itinere Jhierosol.
4to. s. l. et a. (Strassburg, 1468?) *Vide*
de Mas Latrie Histoire de l'ile de Chypre, II., 210.

———————————————— Ed. F. Deycks. 8vo., Stuttgart, 1851

———————————————— Ed. G. A. Neumann (Archives de l'orient
latiu, II., 305). 8vo., Paris, 1884

PICCOLOMINI, ENEA SILVIO, Pope Pius II. De bello Cyprio, id
est caput XCVII. historiæ rerum ubique gestarum in Asia.
Ed. Princeps. Sm. fol., Venice, 1477

BARTHOLOMEO DA LI SONNETTI (ZAMBERTO) Isolario.
4to. (s. l. et a., sed *Venetiis, circa* 1485)

PLANI IO. BAP. In adventum Ser. Catharinæ Corneliæ de Lusignano;
Hier., Cypri et Arm. Reg. Aug. pro S. P. Brixiano oratio.
Absque ulla nota: Sæc. XV.

HUEN, NICOLE LE Relation de pèlerinage en Terre Sainte. (1487–88.)
Fol., Lyon, 1488

SAIGE, JACQUES LE Voyage à Rome . . et autres Saints lieux
(1518). 4to., Cambrai, 1520 and 1523
Ed. R. Duthilloeul, 4to., Douai, 1851

BORDONE, BENEDETTO ISOLARIO, nel quale si ragiona de tutte
l' Isole del Mondo, &c. *Fol.,* Venice, 1528

———————————————— Ricorretto et di nuovo ristam-
pato con la gionta del monte del oro nouamente ritrouato.
Fol., Venice, 1534 and 1547

LE ASSISE Dell' alta Corte del Regno di Hierusalem et Cypro tradute
de Francese in lingua italiana . . . per me Florio Bustron così
comandato da li clariss. Signori Rettori di questo Regno di Cypro.
Fol., Venice, 1535

————————— Assises et bons Usages du Royaume de Jérusalem, tirés
d' un manuscrit de la Bibliothèque Vaticane par messire Jean d' Ibelin
. . . avec des notes et observations et un glossaire . . . par G.
T. de la Thaumassière. *Fol.,* Bourges, 1690

——————— ed. P. Canciani, in " Barbarorum Leges antiquæ."
Fol., 5 vols., Venice, 1781–92

——————— Les livres des Assises et des Usages du reaume de Jerusalem . . ed. E. H. Kausler.
Vol. I., 4to., Stuttgart, 1839

LE ASSISE Assises du Royaume de Jerusalem conférées entre elles, ainsi qu'avec les lois des Francs . . . ed. V. Foucher.

2 parts, 8vo., Rennes, 1839-41

———————— Assises de Jerusalem, ou Recueil des ouvrag s de jurisprudence composés pendant le xIIIme. Siècle dans les Royaumes de Jerusalem et de Chypre. Publiées par M. le Comte Beugnot,

2 vols., fol., Paris, 1843

ANON. Le grand tremblement et epouvantable ruine qui est advenue en la cité de Jerusalem . . avec très grands et merveillabl s vents faictz en la cité de Famagouste, l squels ont été avec grand dommage et ruyne.

(*Plaquette gothique. Ternaux-Compans, Bibl. Asiatique, Paris*, 1841, No. 2830.) *8vo.*, Paris, 1546

———— Ung mervcilleusement grand mouvement de terre . . encore aussi ineffables et horribles vents en l'ile de Chypre en la ville appelée Famagosta et autres places, avec insupportables dommaiges. tr. d' italien en française. (*Plaquette gothique. T.-C.* 2831.)

4to., Anvers, 1546

THEVET ANDRÉ Cosmographie de Levant. *4to.*, Lyon, 1554

———————————— Cosmographie Universelle. (Vol. I., 194-204.)

4to., Lyon, 1575

————————————— Le Grand Insulaire. (With Possot, D. Le voyage de la Terre Sainte, pp. 298-309. Ed. Ch. Schefer.)

Royal 8vo., Paris, 1890

GHISTELE, J. VAN. Voyage van Mhr Joos van Ghistele in den Landen van Slavonien, Griecken, Turckien, Candien, Rhodes en de Cypers. (*Voyage exécuté en* 1481, *décrit par Ambroise Zeebout, Chapelain du Sire de Ghistele.*)

4to., Ghendt, 1557 and 1572

ANON. Les dernières nouvelles de la Victoire des Chrestiens obtenue à l'encontre du Grand Turc . . La desfaicte des Turcs devant Famagosta, ville capitale de Chypre, etc. (*T.-C.* 428.)

8vo., Paris, 1570

AVISI, Gli ultimi circa la guerra che seguita il Turco contra Venetia; Dichiar. molte cose notabili occorse nella Dalmatia, ed in arcipelago, e la Morea. Con il soccorso di Famagosta, etc., 4ff.

8vo., s.l., 1571

CAMOCIO, GIANFRANCESCO Isole famose, porti fortezze sottoposte alla Serenissima Signoria di Venezia.

4to., Venice, 1571

ANON. · Newe Zeitung wie der Türk die Stadt Nicosiam in Cypern dieses verlaufene 1571 Jar eigenommen, auch wie viel tausent Christen er gefangen, etliche tausent gesebelt, was von gemeinem Kriegsvolk gewesen ist, was aber Junker und ansehnliche Leute waren, hat er gen Constantinopel und Alexandria geschieht etlich tausent haben Sich und Weib und Kindt, dass sie den Turken nit in die Handen kamen jemmerlich erstochen und umbbracht.

Wien, 1571

BENEDETTI, ROCCO. Narratio de capta Famagusta, &c.
8vo., Leipzig, 1571

ANON. Cyprus insula a turcico exercitu expugnata. (*T.-C.* 2877.)
Rome, 1571

SOZOMENO, GIO. Narratione della guerra di Nicosia fatta nel Regno di Cipro da' Turchi l'anno 1570.
8vo., Bologna. 1571

ANON. Il crudelissimo assedio e nuova presa della fortezza di Famagosta.
8vo., Milano, 1571

———— Narratio de capta Famagusta : brevis item et vera expositio pugnæ navalis inter Christianos et Turcas apud Echinades.
12mo., Leipzig, 1571

MEMBRE, PHILIP Wahrhaftige und umstendliche Beschreibung wie die Türken anfenglich das treffliche Kœnigreich und Insel Cypern mit grosser Macht überfallen, und darinnen die Hauptstadt Nicosia mit Gewalt erobert. auch folgent solches ausser der eynigen Statt und Port Famagusta unter ihren Gewalt gebracht ; erstlich beschrieben in italienischer Sprach durch Philippum Membre grossen Tollmetsch in turkischer und arabischer Sprach zu Nicosia, und jetzt in teutsch verfertigt sambt einer kurzen Vored und sumarische Beschreibung der Insel Cypern sehr nützlich zu lesen.
4to., (*sine loco, sed*) Nuremberg, 1571

MARTINENGO, NESTORE, COUNT. L'assedio et presa di Famagosta, dove s'intende minutissimamente le scaramuccie e batterie, mine et assalti dati ad essa fortezza.
8vo., Verona, 1572

———————————————— Relatione di tutto il successo di Famagosta . . . fortezza.
4to., Venice, 1572

————————————————— L'Intiero Ragguaglio del successo di Famagosta, dove minutamente s'intendono tutti gli abbatimenti et assalti dal principio della guerra infino alla resa di essa città a patti non servati.
4to., Venice ? 1572 ?

————————————————— Wahrhaftige Relation und Bericht was massen die gewaltige Stadt und Befestigung Famagusta in Cipro so von mœnniklich für ganz ungewünnlich gehalten, von den Turken im August des 1571 Jars mit unerhoerten Gewalt erobert und eingenommen worden . . . durch ein gutherziger aus welscher sprach in teutsch transferirt.
4to., (*Sine loco et anno.* Vide *Meusel, Bibl. Hist. II. Pars I. p.* 105)

————————————————— The true Report of all the suecesse of Famagosta, of the antique writers called Tamassus, a citie in Cyprus . . . Englished out of Italian by Willian Malim with a short description also of his of the same Island.
4to., London, 1572
Fol., *ibid.*, 1599

————————————————— La vrai histoire du Siège et de la prinse de Famagosta l'une des principalles villes du royaume de Chypre . . . escrite en Italien par le Seigneur Nestor Martinengo Capitaine des compagnies qui estoyent dedant . . . et puis mise en françois.
8vo,, Paris, 1572

ANON. Famagusta, Sampt ihrer Belagerung und Eroberung.
(*T.-C.* 2881.) *4to.*, Nürnberg. 1572

———— Famagusta, wie es allenthalben mit derselben Stadt ergangen.
(*T.-C.* 2882.) *4to.*, 1573

COMES NATALIS (NATALE CONTI). Historia snorum temporum,
libri, **x.** *4to.*, Venice, 1572

———————————— Historia snorum temporum, libri **xxx.**
4to., Venice, 1581

CONTI NATALE. Le istorie dei suoi tempi, tralotte da Giancarlo
Saraceni sopra l'originale latino accresciuto dall'autore prima della
morte. Venice, 1589

MANOLESSO, EMILIO M. Historia nova, nella quale si contengono
tutti i successi della guerra Turchesca . . . e finalmente tutto
quello che nel mondo è occorso da l' anno MDLXX. fino all'hora
presente. *4to.*, Padua, 1572

CONTARINI, GIO. P. Historia della cose successe dal principio della
guerra mossa da Selim Ottomano à Venetiani fino al di della gran
giornata vittoriosa contra Turchi.
4to., Venice, 1572, 12*mo.*, Milan, 1572
8*vo.*, Venice, 1645

————————————— Historia von dem Krieg welchen neulich der
Türchisch Keiser Selim der ander wider die Venediger erreget hat. Von
G. Henisch verteutschet. *4to.*, Basel, 1573

HERRERA, FERNAND DE Relacion de la guerra de Chypre y
suceso de la Batalla Naval de Lepanto. 8*vo.*, Seville, 1572

LUSIGNANO, FR. STEFFANO di Cipro, dell' ordine de Predicatori.
Chorograffia et breve Historia universale dell' isola de Cipro princi-
piando al tempo di Noë per in sino al 1572. *4to.*, Bologna, 1572

———————————— Description de toute l'Isle de Chypre.
4to., Paris, 1580

———————————— Raccolta di cinque discorsi, intitolati
Corone, per comprender in se cose appartenenti a gran Rè et a Principi.
4to., Padova, 1577

———————————— Histoire Générale des royaumes de
Hierusalem, Chypre, Arménie et lieux circonvoisins.
4to., Paris, 1613

———————————— Les droits autoritez et prérogatives
que prétendent au royaume de Hierusalem les princes et seigneurs
spirituels et temporels, savoir, le Pape, Patriarches, Empereurs, Rois
de France, Angleterre, Aragon, Naples, Hongrie, Cypre et Arménie,
&c. *4to.*, Paris, 1586

CALEPIO, ANGELO Vera et fidelissima narratione del successo dell'
espugnatione, e defensione del regno di Cipro. (*pp.* 92–124 *of Fr. S.
Lusignano's* Chorograffia, *Bologna*, 1573.)

CALEPIEN, FRERE ANGE De la prinse de Nicosie, 1570. (*printed
at the end of Fr. E. Lusignan's* Histoire Générale, *Paris*, 1613.)

BIZZARRI, PIETRO   La Vraye Histoire du Siège de Famagoste.
Sm. 8*vo.*, Paris, 1572

———————— ——— Cyprium Bellum inter Venetos et Selymum Turco-
rum Imperatorem gestum : libris tribus descriptum.
8*vo.*, Basle, 1573

———————————— Histoire de la guerre qui s'est passée entre les
Venetiens et la Sainte Ligue contre les Turcs pour l'Isle de Cypre
ès années 1570, 1571, 1572 : mise en français par F. de Belleforest.
Sm. 8*vo.*, Paris, 1573

PORCACCHI DA CASTIGLIONE, THOMASO   L'Isole piu famose
del mondo.   *Sm. fol.*, Venice, 1576, 1590 and 1605
Padua, 1620

FAROLDO, JULIO   Annali Veneti.   8*vo.*, Venice, 1577

NORES, GIASON DI   Orazione al Doge Sebastiano Veniero per nome
di quei gentiluomini del regno di Cipro che dopo la perdita della
patria si trovavano presenti al tempo della sua creazione.
4*to.*, Padua, 1578

ANON.   Historie et genealogie des princes et grands seigneurs dont la
plupart étoient françois qui ont commandé ez royaumes de Hierusalem,
Cypre, Arménie et autres lieux circonvoisins.   (*T.-C.* 2889.)
4*to.*, Paris, 1579

GIUSTI, VINC.   Irene.   Tragedia nova.   12*mo.*, Venice, 1580

METELLI, VINC. GIUSTINOPOLITANO   Il Marte : sotto bellisime
favole et inventioni si descrive tutta la guerra di Cipro con la lotta
dell' armata de' turchi.   4*to.*, Venice, 1582

SALIGNAC, BART. DE   Itinerarium Hierosolymitarum (1517).
8*vo.*, Magdeburg, 1587

FULIGNI, VALERIO   Bragadino ; tragedia.   8*vo.*, Pesaro, 1589

SILVESTRANI—BRENZONE, CR.   Vita e fatti del valorosissimo
capitano Astorre Baglione da Perugia con la guerra di Cipro.
4*to.*, Verona, 1591

——————— ——————————— ———— La guerra di Cypro di cui
generale era Astorre Baglione, et si descrive tutta quell'Isola.
(*Ristampa dell'opera del Silvestrani dal cap. VIII. al XX.*)
4*to.*, Lucerne, 1646

ANON.   La Loyssée, contenant le voyage de Saint Louis, roi de France,
pour aller en Egypte contre les Sarrazins, son embarquement et son
arrivée en l'Isle de Chypre, et adventures survenues.   (*T.-C.* 666.)
4*to.*, Blois, 1593

FOLIETTA, UBERTUS   De cansis magnitudinis Imperii turcici ac narratio belli Cyprii inter Venetos et Turcas superioribus annis gesti.
12*mo.*, Leipzig, 1594

——————————————— Istoria di Mons. UBERTO FOGLIETTA nobile
Genovese della sacra Lega contra Selim, e d'alcune altre imprese di
suoi tempi . . . fatta volgare da Giulio Guastavini.
4*to.*, Genoa, 1598

ANON. Trattato delle ragioni sopra il regno di Cipro, con narratione d' historia del violento spoglio commesso dal bastardo Giacomo Lusignano. *4to.*, Torino, 1594

BAUMGARTEN, MARTIN Peregrinatio in Ægyptum, Arabiam, &c.
4to., Nürnberg, 1594

———————————————— Travels (a collection of Voyages and Travels).
London, *fol.*, 1704, and 8*vo.*, 175'’

GUARNERIUS, IO. ANT. De bello Cyprio, libri tres.
4to., Bergamo, 1597

———————————————— Nunc denuo excusi. *4to.*, Bergamo, 1602

ROSACCIO, GIUSEPPE Viaggio da Venetia a Constantinopoli per mare e per terra, insieme quello di Terra Santa.
Obl. 8vo.. Venice, 1598 and 1606

VILLAMONT, JACQUES DE Les voyages du Seigneur de Villamont.
8*vo.*, Paris, 1598, 16*mo.*, Arras, 1598

(and many later editions, Paris, Arras, Lyon, Rouen, 1600–1698.)

HAKLUYT, R. Principal navigations, voyages, traffiques and discoveries of the English nation. 3 *rols.*, *fol.*, London, 1599

CARR, RALPH The Mahumetane or Turkish historie . . . a brief discourse of the warres of Cypres. *4to.*, London, 1600

EHINGEN GEORG VON Itinerarium ; das ist : Historische Beschreibung, weilung Herrn G. V. Ehingen's Raisens nach der Ritterschaft von 150 Jaren in X underschidliche Königreich verbracht.
Fol., Augsburg, 1600

PARUTA, PAOLO Historia Vinetiana, divisa in due parti. Nelle parte seconda in due libri si contiene la Guerra fatta dalla Lega de' Prencipi Christiani contra Selimo Ottomano per occasione del Regno di Cipro.
4to., Vinetia, 1605

———————————————— Storia della Guerra di Cipro, Libri tre.
8*vo.*, Siena, 1827

———————————————— The History of Venice . . . likewise the wars of Cyprus . . . wherein the famous sieges of Nicossia and Famagosta, and battel of Lepanto are contained. Made English by Henry, Earl of Monmouth. 2 *parts*, *fol.*, London, 1658

KNOLLES, RICHARD The general Historie of the Turks, &c.
Fol., London, 1603
2*nd ed. fol.*, London, 1610
3*rd ed. fol.*, London, 1621
6th ed. (continued by Sir P. Rycaut.) 3 *rols.*, *fol.*, London, 1687–1700
(Abridged by W. Savage.) 2 *vols.*, 8*vo.*, 1701

SANDYS, GEORGE A relation of a journey begun in 1610. Foure bookes, containing a description of the Turkish Empire.
Fol., London, 1615
(and seven other editions between 1621 and 1673.)

PALERNE, JEAN Pèregrinations. 12*mo.*, Lyon, 1606

BEAUVAU, HENRI DE   Relation journaliere du voyage du Levant.
4to., Nancy, 1615

COTOVICUS, JOANNES (JOHANN VAN KOOTWYCK) Itinerarium Hierosolymitanum et Syriacum. in quo variarum gentium mores et instituta, &c., recensentur : acc. synopsis reipublicæ Venetæ.
4to., Antwerp, 1619

BOSIO, GIACOMO   Dell' Istoria della Sacra Religione et Illustrissima militia di San Giovanni Gerosolomitano.
Fol. Vol. I., Roma, 1621, *Vol. II.*, Roma, 1630, *Vol. III.*, Napoli, 1684.

FAVYN, ANDRÉ Le Theâtre d'honneur et de chevalerie, etc.
4to., Paris, 1620

FAVYN, AND.   The Theatre of Honour and Knighthood. (Book IX., pp. 361–373. The order of Cyprus, and of Luzignan, called of the Sword. Instituted in the year MCLXXXXV. by Guye of Luzignan, King of Jerusalem, and of Cyprus.) Translated from the French.
Fol., London, 1623

NEUMAYR, J. W.   Bellum Cypricum, oder Beschreibung des Krieges welchen 1570–2 des gross Türk Selim wider die Venetianer wegen des Konigreichs Cypern geführet. *Sm. 4to.*, Leipzig, 1621

FURER VON HAIMENDORF CHR.   Itinerarium Ægypti, etc. (1566.) *4to.*, Nuremberg, 1621

D. C. LE SIEUR (LOUIS DES HAYES, BARON DE COURMENIN) Voiage de Levant, fait par le commandement du Roy en l'année 1621.
4to., Paris, 1624 and 1645

GRAZIANI, A. M.   Antonii Mariæ Gratiani a Burgo Sancti Sepulcri Episcopi Amerini de Bello Cyprio libri cinque.
4to., Roma, 1624

———————— Histoire de la guerre de Chypre écrite en latin . . et traduite en français par M. Le Peletier.   *4to.*, Paris 1685

———————— *Idem*   2 *vols.*, 12mo., Lyon, 1686

———————— The History of the War of Cyprus. (Translated by Robert Midgley.)   *8vo.*, London, 1687

———————— The Sieges of Nicosia and Famagusta, with a sketch of the earliest history of Cyprus. Ed. from Midgley by C. D. Cobham.
8vo., London. 1900

PURCHAS, SAMUEL   Purchas his Pilgrimes.
4 *vols., fol.*, London, 1625

BRÉVES, FR. S. DE   Relation des Voyages . . . faits en Jéru-salem (1604).   *4to.*, Paris, 1628 and 1630

MONODO, RIETRO   Trattato del titolo regio dovuto alla Serenissima Casa di Savoia insieme con un ristretto delle Rivolutioni del Reame di Cipri appartenente alla Corona dell A. R. di Vittorio Amadeo Duca di Savoia, Principe di Piemonte, Re di Cipri.
Fol., Turin, 1633

GIANNOTTI, GASPARO Parere . . sopra il Ristretto delle revoluzioni del reame di Cipri e ragioni della Serenissima Casa di Savoia sopra esso, insieme con un breve trattato del titolo regale dovuto a S. A. S. stampati in Torino senza nome d'autore. (*Monodo Pietro*.)
Fol., Francofort, 1633

MEURSIUS, J. FIL. Majestas Veneta sive de Scr. Reip. cum in Creta, tum in Cypro, titulo regio, hone jure vindicato contra anonymum dissertatio. 12*mo.*, Leyden, 1640

STOCHOVE, LE SIEUR DE, Voyage faict ès années 1630-33.
4*to.*, Bruxelles, 1643 and 1650 and 12*mo.*, Rouen, 1670

WILBRAND VON OLDENBURG Peregrinatio (1211).
8*vo.*, Cologne, 1653

———————————————————————— Ed. J. C. M Laurent (Peregrinatores medii ævi quatuor). 4*to.*, Leipzig, 1864 and 1873

ASSARINO, LUCA Ragguagli del Ileguo di Cipro.
12*mo.*, Bologna, 1642 and Venice, 1654

ANON. Svegliarino. che mostra alla Chrisziánità essere gionta l'bora opportuna di mouersi contro la Potenza Ottomana esposto in publico da G.B.C.V. 4*to.*, Lucerne, 1646

LOREDANO, GIO. FR. Historic de' Rè Lusignani publicate da Henrico Giblet Cavalier, libri undeci. 4*to.*, Bologna, 1647
12*mo.*, 1653 and 1660

———————————————————————— Histoire des Rois de Chypre de la Maison de Lusignan . . traduit de l'Italien du Chevalier Giblet, Cypriot.
2 *vols.*, 16*mo.*, Paris, 1732

NEOPHYTUS, RHODINUS Περὶ ἡρώων στρατηγῶν . . . ὅπου εὐγήκασιν ἀπὸ τὸ ι ησὶ Κύπρου. 12*mo.*, Rome, 1659

SOMER, JAN Zee en Landt Reyse gedaen naer de Levante als Italien, Candien, Cypres, e.z.v. 4*to.*, Amsterdam, 1661

DELLA VALLE, PIETRO De' Viaggi. (Parte terza, pp. 438-453.)
4*to.*, Rome, 1663

GERASIMOS CHRISTOPHOROU Ἀκολουθία τοῦ ὁσίου καὶ θεοφόρου πατρὸς ἡμῶν 'Ιωάννου τοῦ Λαμπαδιστοῦ.
4*to.*, Venice, 1667

MEURSIUS, J. Creta, Cyprus, Rhodus.
Sm. 4to., Amstelodami, 1675

—————————— Opera. (*In* 12 *vols. fol., Florence.* 1741-63, *on pp.* 545-679 of Vol. iii. is*)* Cyprus, sive de illins insulæ rebus et antiquitatibus.
Fol., Florence, 1744

MEDICI, GIACOMO Catterina Cornaro, Opera comica.
8*vo.*, Udine, 1675

ABUDACNUS, JOS. Historia Jacobitarum seu Coptorum in Ægypto . et Cypri insulæ parte habitantium.
4*to.*, Oxford, 1675, and 8*vo.*, Leiden, 1740

RICAUT, PAUL The present state of the Greek and Armenian Churches.
8*vo.*, London, 1679

PHILIPPI CYPRII   Chronicon Ecclesiæ Græcæ.   Gr. et Lat.
4*to.*, Franequeræ, 1679

NEOPHYTUS   (Cir. A.D. 1200.)   Περὶ τῶν κατὰ χῶραν Κύπρου σκαιῶν.
(In Cotelerius, Eccl. Gr. Mon. vol. ii.)   4*to.*, Paris, 1681
and see also Rolls Series Publications, 38A. pp. clxxxi-ix.
8*vo.*, London, 1864

——— ——— An account of the "Misfortunes of Cyprus" by Neophytus, and the condition of the Island in his time, by Edwin
Freshfield. (Archæologia, vol. xlvii.)
4*to.*, Westminster, 1881

——— ——— ᾽Ακολουθίαι τοῦ ὁσίου Πατρὸς ἡμῶν Νεοφύτου τοῦ
ἐγκλείστου.   4*to.*, Venice, 1778
῎Εκδοσις ἑευτέρα.   4*to.*, Nicosia, 1893

——— ——— Τυπικὴ διάταξις καὶ λόγοι εἰς τὴν ῾Εξαήμερον.
4*to.*, Venice, 1779

——— ——— The "Ritual Ordinance."   Ed. F. E. Warren.
(Archæologia, vol. xlvii.)   4*to.*, Westminster, 1881

PIACENZA,   FRANC.   L'Egeo redivivo o sia Chorographia dell' Arcipelago   di Candia e Cipri.   4*to.*, Modena, 1688

DAPPER, O.   Naukeurige Beschryving der Eilanden in de Archipel der
Middelantsche Zee.   4*to.* Amsterdam, 1688

——— ——— Description exacte des isles de l'archipel . . traduite du
Flamand.   *Fol.*, Amsterdam, 1703

CORONELLI,   VICENZO   Atlante Veneto . . ad uso dell' Accade-
mia cosmografica degli Argonauti.   *Fol.*, Venice, 1692

NODOT,   FRANC.   Histoire de Mélusine tirée des chroniques de Poitou, et
qui sert d'origine à l'ancienne maison de Lusignan,
12*mo.*, Paris, 1698

BRUYN,   C.   DE   Reisen door de vermaadste Deelen van Klein Asia, de
Eylanden Scio, Rhodus, Cyprus, &c.   *Fol.*, Delft, 1698

——— ——— Voyage à travers les pates les plus fameuses de
l'Asie Mineure, les iles de Scio, Rhodes, Chypre, &c.
Fol., Delft, 1700 ; Paris, 1714

——— ——— A Voyage to the Levant, or Travels in . . the Islands
Scio, Rhodes, Cyprus, &c.   Done into English by W. J.
Fol., London, 1702

——— ——— ——— Voyage en Levant c'est-à-dire dans les principaux endroits
de l'Asie Mineure, dans les isles de Chio, Rhodes, Chypre. &c.
5 *vols.*, 4*to.*, Paris, 1725 ; La Haye, 1732

SAGREDO,   JEAN   Histoire de l'Empire Ottoman.
7 *vols.*, 8*vo.*, Paris, 1724

MERCADO, P.   Νέα ἐγκυκλοπαιδεία τῆς ἀποστολῆς τῆς Κύπρου.   (Nova
Encyclopædia missionis apostolicæ in Regno Cypri—*also entitled*
Institutiones Linguæ Græcæ–Vulgaris.   4*to.*, Rome, 1732

ANON.   Gregorii Cypri Vita.   4*to.*, Venice, 1753

DRUMMOND, ALEX. Travels through different cities of Germany, Italy, Greece. and several parts of Asia. *Fol.*, London, 1754

LE QUIEN, MICHEL Oriens Christianus. 3 *vols.*, *fol.*, Paris, 1740

POCOCKE, RICHARD A description of the East and some other countries. 2 *vols.*, *fol.*, London, 1743-45

———————————— Voyages en Orient, traduit de l'anglois sur la seconde edition par Eydous. 6 *vols.*, 12*mo.*, Neuchatel, 1772

———————————— Beschreibung des Morgenlandes u.s.w., a.d. Eng. übersetzt von C. E. von Windheim. 3 parts in two volumes.
4to., Erlangen, 1754-55

———————————— Id. übersetzt und mit Anmerkungen von Schreber. 3 *vols.*. *4to.*, Erlangen, 1771-3

NIEBUHR, CARSTEN Reisen durch Syrien und Palæstina, nach Cypern u.s.w.
3 *vols.*, *4to.*, Copenhagen, 1744, and Hamburg, 1837

JAUNA, DOM. Histoire générale des Roiaumes de Chypre, de Jerusalem, &c. 2 *vols.*, *4to.*, Leiden, 1747 and 1785

DIEDO, GIACOMO Storia della Republica di Venezia dalla sua fondazione sino l'anno 1747. 4 *vols.*, *4to.*, Venice, 1751

EPHRAIM, Patriarch of Jerusalem. Περιγραφὴ τῆς ἱερᾶς σεβασμίας καὶ βασιλικῆς μονῆς τοῦ Κύκκου. *4to.*, Venice, 1751 and 1782
3rd. ed., 1817, 4th. ed., *4to.*, Venice, 1819

———————————— Ἀζὴμ πατησσὰχ μοναστὴρ ΚΥΚΚΟΝΟΥΝ χεκμετλοῦ βασιτουλλὰχ εἰκόνα ταπφηροῦν, χαγιρλὴ πηνγαροῦν χεκμετναμὲ ταριχὴ πεανηντάτηρ. (*A Turkish version of the above. printed in Greek character.*) *4to.*, Venice, 1816

———————————— Τυπικὴ ιιάταξις. (Ritual Ordinance of the founder Nilus (**A.D.** 1200) for the Monastery of the Blessed Virgin of Machæra.)
8*vo.*, Venice, 1756

———————————— Βίβλος περιέχουσα κανόνας μερικῶν τινων Ἁγίων μετὰ καὶ προτροπῆς τινος πρὸς τοὺς ἐν Κύκκῳ Πατέρας.
4to., Venice, 1756

———————————— Ἀκολουθία τοῦ Ἁγίου ἐνδόξου Ἀπ. Βαρνάβα.
4to., Venice, 1756

EGMOND VAN DER NYENBURG, J. Æ. and **J. HEYMAN** Reizen door een gedeelte van Europa Klein Asien, verscheide Eilanden van de Archipel, Syrien . . briefsgewyse samengestelt door Joh. W. Ch. Heyman. 2 *vols.*, *4to.*, Leiden, 1757-8

———————————— Travels through . . the Islands of the Archipelago. Translated from the Low Dutch.
2 *vols.*, 8*vo.*, London, 1759

HASSELQUIST, DR. FR. Reise nach Palästina in den Jahren 1749-52. (From the Swedish.) 8*vo.*, Rostock, 1762

———————————— Voyages and Travels in the Levant, in the years 1749-52. 8*vo.*, London, 1766

HASSELQUIST, Dr. FR. Voyages dans le Levant . . . trad. de l' allemand. 12mo., Paris, 1769

ARRIGHI, ANT. M. De bello Cyprio, Libri V. 4to., Padua, 1764

GERMANUS, Patriarch of Constantinople. Two letters to the Cypriots. (Cotelerius, Mon. Ecc. Græcæ, II., 475, and) Reinhard, I., Beylagen, pp 16-37.) 4to., Erlangen, 1766

REINHARD, J. P. Vollständige Geschichte des Königreichs Cypern.
2 vols., 4to., Erlangen, 1766 and 1768

BRYENNIOS, JOSEPH Ἰωσὴφ Μοναχοῦ τοῦ Βρυεννίου τὰ εὑρεθέντα . . . ἤδη τὸ πρῶτον τύποις ἐκδοθέντα.
2 vols., 8vo., Leipzig, 1768

SAVORGNANO, ASCANIO Copiosa descrizione delle cose di Cipro con le ragioni in favor, o contra diverse opinioni, e delle provisioni necessarie per quel Regno. (Ex M.Sto in Reinhard's Geschichte der K. Cypern, Vol. II., Beylagen, pp: 33-53.) 4to., Erlangen, 1768

DIFESA, Delle ragioni e Maestà della Ser. Republica di Venezia contro il libro publicato a nome de' Savoiardi. (Ex M.Sto in Reinhard's Geschichte des Königreich's Cypern, Vol. II., Beylagen, pp. 158-214.)
4to., Erlangen, 1768

MARITI, GIO. Viaggi per l'isola di Cipro, &c. . .
5 vols., 8vo., Lucca, 1769

———————— Reisen durch die Insel Cypern . . in einem Auszug aus dem Italienischen übersetzt von Ch. G. Hase.
8vo., Altenburg, 1777

———————— Voyages dans l'Isle de Chypre, &c.
2 vols., 8vo., Neuwied and Paris, 1791

———————— Travels through Cyprus, Syria and Palestine.
2 vols., 8vo., London, 1791

———————— Travels in the Island of Cyprus. Translated by C. D. Cobham. 8vo., Nicosia, 1895

———————— Del vino di Cipro, Ragionamento (dedicated to Nassau, 3rd Earl Cowper). 12mo., Florence, 1772

———————— Dissertazione sopra la Città di Citium nell' isola di Cipro.
8vo., Livorno, 1787

———————— Viaggio de Gerusalemme per le Coste della Soria. (Vide Vol. II., pp. 129-171.) 2 vols., 8vo., Livorno, 1787

D'ANVILLE, J. B. Recherches géographiques sur l'île de Chypre. (Géographie ancienne abrégée.) Fol., Paris, 1769
———————— Compendium of ancient geography.
2 vol., 8vo., London, 1810

MACARIOS, Bishop of Citium. Ἀκολουθία τοῦ ἁγίου ἱερομάρτυρος Ἑρμογένους τοῦ Θαυματουργοῦ. 4to., Venice, 1772

CHRYSANTHOS, Archbishop of Cyprus. Ἀκολουθία τοῦ ἐν Ἁγίοις πατρός ἡμῶν Ἡρακλειδίου, ἐπισκόπου Ταμασέων.
4to., Venice, 1774

CHRYSANTHOS, Archbishop of Cyprus. Ἀκολουθία τοῦ ἐν Ἁγίοις πατρὸς ἡμῶν Μνάσωνος, ἐπισκόπου Ταμασέων.

4to., Venice, 1774

――――――― Ἀκολουθίαι τῶν ὁσίων Ἀναστασίου, Χαρίτωνος, Αὐξεντίου καὶ Κενδέα. Τοῦ Ἀπ. καὶ Εὐγγ. Λουκᾶ, τοῦ Ἁγ. Δημητριάνου Κυθήρης, καὶ Κωνσταντίνου μάρτυρος. 8vo., Venice, 1779

KORTE, JONAS Reize naar Palestina, Egypte, Phenicie, Syrie, Mesopotamic en Cypris uit het hoogduitsche.

2 vols., 8vo., Haarlem, 1776

FORMALEONI, Catterina Regina di Cipro. Tragedia in cinque atti, in verso sciolto. 8vo., Venice, 1783

ANON. A Journal kept on a journey from Bassora to Bagdad, over the little desert, to Aleppo, Cyprus, Rhodes, &c., 1779.

8vo., Horsham, 1784

KYPRIANOS, ARCHIMANDRITE Ἱστορία χρονολογικὴ τῆς νήσου Κύπρου. 4to., Venice, 1788

―――――――――――― Do. 4to., Latnaea, 1880
(The first book printed in Cyprus.)

PHILOTHEOS, Archbishop of Cyprus. Σημειώσεις περὶ τῆς τῶν Κυπρίων ἐκκλησίας, καὶ ἔκθεσις αὐτοῦ περὶ τῶν προνομίων τῆς αὐτῆς· ἔτει 1740. (In Kyprianos' History, pp. 370-390.)

4to., Venice, 1788

MICHAEL, Abp. of Cyprus. Ἀκολουθία τοῦ Ἁγίου ἱερομάρτυρος Θεράποντος τοῦ Θαυματουργοῦ. 8vo., Venice, 1801

SONNINI, C. S. Voyage en Grèce et en Turquie.
2 vols., 8vo., Paris, An. IX., 1801, London, 1801

OLIVIER, G. A. Voyage dans l'Empire Ottoman.
3 vols., 4to., Paris, 1801-07

WERNER, F. L. Z. Die Templer auf Cypern, dramatisches Gedicht.
Berlin, 1803

―――――――――― The Templars in Cyprus : a dramatic poem. Translated by E. A. M. Lewis. Post 8vo., London, 1886

MAYER, LUIGI Views in the Ottoman Empire, chiefly in Caramania, the islands of Rhodes and Cyprus. . with historical observations and incidental illustrations of the manners and customs of the natives of the country. Fol., London, 1803

AINSLIE, ROBERT Views in the Ottoman Empire . . . with some curious selections from the islands of Rhodes and Cyprus.

4to., London, 1803

VEZIN, MICHAEL DE Nachrichten über Aleppo und Cypern aus dem noch ungedruckten englischen original-handschrift übersetzt und heraus gegeben von D. Harles. (In Sprengel's Bibliothek der neuesten und wichtigsten Reisebeschreibungen.) Weimar, 1804

LENZ, C. G. Die Göttin von Paphos auf alten Bildwerken.
Gotha, 1808

CLARKE, E. D. Travels in various countries of Europe, Asia and Africa. (Cyprus, Part II., Section 1, pp. 308-356.)

6 *vols.*, 4*to.*, Cambridge and London, 1810-23

———————— Voyages en Russie, en Tartarie et en Turquie, trad. de l'Anglais.

3 *vols.*, 8*vo.*, Paris, 1813

HAMMER-PURGSTALL, JOS. BARON VON Topographische Ansicht-en auf einer Reise in die Levante.

4*to.*, Wien. 1811

———————————————— Geschichte des Osman-ischen Reiches.

10 *vols.*, 8*vo.*, Pest, 1827-35

——————————————— Histoire de l'Empire Ottoman, trad. de l'Allemand par J. J. Hellert. (Vol. VI., pp. 383-418.)

18 *vols.*, 8*vo.*, Paris, 1835-43

——————————————— Histoire de l'Empire Ottoman, trad. de l'Allemand sur la 2e ed. par M. Dochez.

3 *vols.*, 8*vo.*, Paris, 1840-42

BERGK, J. A. Ansichten v.d. Turkei . . Rhodus, Cypern. &c.

Fol., Leipzig, 1812

ALI BEY, EL ABBASSI Voyages en Afrique et en Asie, 1803-6.

3 *vols.*, 8*vo.*, Paris, 1814

· ——————————— Travels in Morocco, Tripoli, Cyprus, &c.

2 *vols.*, 4*to.*, London, 1816

————————————· Viatjes per Africa y Assia durante los anuos 1803-1807.

8*vo.*, Barcelona, 1889

WALPOLE, ROBERT Memoirs relating to European and Asiatic Turkey.

4*to.*, London, 1816

——————————— Travels in various countries in the East.

4*to.*, London, 1820

CORANCEZ, L.A.O. DE Itinéraire.

8*vo.*, Paris, 1816

LIGHT, CAPT. H., R.A. Travels in Egypt, &c., and Cyprus in 1814.

4*to.*, London, 1818

HAJI KHALFA (Katib Chelebi). Jihan Name. Geografia orientalis. Ex Turcico in Latinum versa a Matth. Norberg.

8*vo.*, Gotha, 1818

——————————— " Kitab tuhfet el kibar fi asfar el bihar."

4*to.*, Constantinople, 1828

——————————— History of the maritime wars of the Turks, translated from the Turkish by J. Mitchell.

4*to.*, London, 1831

KINNEIR, J. M. Journey through Asia Minor, &c., 1813-14.

8*vo.*, London, 1818

——————————— Voyage dans l'Asie Mineure, &c. Trad. de l'Anglais par M. Perrin.

2 *vols.*, 8*vo.*, Paris, 1818

CONSTANTIUS, Archbishop of Sinai. Κυπριὰς χαρίεσσα καὶ ἐπίτομος. (Printed with the Περιγραφὴ τῆς μονῆς τοῦ Κύκκου.)

4*to.*, Venice, 1819

TURNER, W.   Journal of a Tour in the Levant.

3 vols., 8*vo.*, London. 1820

RICHTER, O. F. VON   Wallfahrten in Morgenlande.

Berlin, 1822

RAFFENEL, H.   Des évènements de la Gréce.

8*vo.*, Paris, 1822

POUQUEVILLE, F. C. H. L.   Histoire de la Régénération de la Grèce, comprenant le précis des évènements depuis 1740 jusqu'en 1824.

4 vols., 8*vo.*, Paris, 1824

MUNTER, Bp. FRED.   Der Tempel der himmlischen Göttin zu Paphos.   4*to.*, Copenhagen, 1824

GUIGNIAUT, J. B.   La Venus de Paphos et son temple.

8*vo.*, Paris, 1827

SILBERMANN, G.   Notice sur Tschélèbi Hadji Pétraki, ancien Primat du District de Cythérée dans l'ile de Chypre.

12*mo.*, Strasbourg, 1827

FRANKLAND, Capt. C. C.   Travels   to Cyprus, Syria, &c., in 1827 and 1828.   *2 vols.*, 8*vo.*, London, 1830

DELAROIÈRE, M.   Voyage en Orient,   (Chypre, pp. 41-44.)

8*vo.*, Paris, 1836

FIORIO, GIR.   La Regina di Cipro.   Romanzo storico.

8*vo* , Mantova, 1838

ENGEL, W. H.   Kypros.   Eine Monographie.

2 vols., 8*vo.*, Berlin, 1841

EMO, GIO.   Caterina Cornelia Regina di Cipro.

8*vo.*, Venice, 1843

RICCOBONI, ANT.   Historia de Salamina capta et M. Antonio Bragadeno præside excoriato.   (Nozze Arrigoni-Luccheschi.)

8*vo.*, Venice, 1843

FABER, FR. FELIX   Evagatorium in Terræ Sanctæ, Arabiæ et Egypti preregrinationem.   (1484.)   Ed. C. D. Hassler.

3 vols., 8*vo.*, Stuttgart, 1843-49

WILDE, Sir W. R. W.   Narrative of a Voyage . . . along the shores of the Mediterranean, including a visit   to Cyprus.

8*vo.*, Dublin, 1844

THEISS, CARLO   Dissertatio de bello Cyprio.

4*to.*, Nordhusæ, 1844

ALEARDI, G. ALEARDO   Arnalda. (*An episode in the siege of* *Nicosia.*)   12*mo.*, Milan, 1844

POCH, IOS.   Enumeratio plantarum hucusque cognitarum insulæ Cipri.   Vienna, 1844

SACCHERA, —.   Catterina Cornaro.   Musica di Donizetti.

12*mo.*, Milan

ANON. Investitura del Regno di Cipro, data dal Soldano d' Egitto alla Regina Caterina Cornaro. (Archivio Storico Italiano, Serie I., Vol, VIII., parte II.. p. 605.) *8vo.*, Firenze, 1845

SERENO, BART. Commentari della Guerra di Cipro e della Lega dei principi cristiani contró il Turco.
Royal 8vo., Monte Cassino, 1845

PAGANO, MARIO Delle imprese e del dominio dei Genovesi nella Grecia. *8vo.*, Genoa, 1846

TOMITANO, BERNARDINO · L'assedio e presa di Nicosia addi 9 Settembre, 1570. (Nozze Campano—Gröller.) *4to.*, Padua, 1846

——————————————— Resa di Famagosta, e fine lagrimevole di Bragadino e di Astorre Baglioni. (Brano storico pubb. da A. Ruzzini per nozze Marcello—Zon. *8vo.*, Venice, 1858

GUIDI, FR. La Regina di Cipro. Dramma lirico in 4 atti. Musica di G. Pacini. *12mo.*, Milan, 1846

ROSS, LUDWIG Assyrisches Basrelief auf Cypern. (Hellenica, I., i. pp. 69, 70, with plate.) *4to.*, Halle, 1846

————————————— Reisen nach Kos, Halikarnassos, und der Insel Cypern. *4 vols.*, *8vo.*, Halle, 1852

MAS LATRIE, L. COMTE DE Relation politiques et commerciales de l'Asie Mineure avec d'île de Chypre au moyen age. (Bibl. de l'école de Chartes, 2e série. tom, i. et iii.)
8vo., Paris. 1844-6

——————————————— Rapport addressé à M. le Ministre de l'Instruction publique. *8vo.*, Paris, 1846

——————————————— Nicosie, ses souvenirs historiques et sa situation présente. (Extract du Correspondant, t. xvii. 25 Juin et 10 Août, 1847, p. 505 et 852.) *8vo.*, Paris, 1847

——————————————— Premier rapport à M. le Ministre de l'Instruction publique. (Archives des Missions Scientifiques. t. i., 502.) Paris, 1850

——————————————— Notice sur la situation actuelle de l'île de Chypre, et sur la construction d'une carte de l'île. (Archives des Missions Scientifiques, t. i. 161.) Paris, 1850

——————————————— Description des églises de construc-tion française dans l'île de Chypre. *8vo.*, Paris, 1850

——————————————— Histoire de l'île de Chypre sous le Règne des Princes de la Maison de Lusignan. *3 vols.*, *royal 8vo.*, Paris, *vol. II.*, 1852, *vol. III.*, 1855, *vol. I.*, 1861

——————————————— Note (*Notice* 1863) sur la construc-tion d'une Carte de l'île de Chypre. *8vo.*, Paris, 1862

——————————————— Nouvelles preuves de l'histoire de Chypre sous le Règne des princes de la maison de Lusignan. (Bibl. de l'école des Chartès, t. 32 et 34, Réunies en un volume.)
8vo., Paris, 1873

MAS LATRIE, L. COMTE DE Guillaume de Machaut et la prise d' Alexandrie. (Extr. de la Bibl. de l'Ec. des Chartes.)

8*vo*., Paris, 1876

———————————————— Jacques II. de Lusignan archevêque de Nicosie et ses premiers successeurs. (Extr. de la Bibl. de l'Ec. des Chartes, t. xxxviii.) 8*vo*., Paris,

———————————————— L'île de Chypre, sa situation présente et ses souvenirs du moyen age. 12mo., Paris, 1879

———————————————— Généalogie des Rois de Chypre de la famille de Lusignan. (Extrait de l'Archivio Veneto.) Venice, 1881

———————————————— Généalogie. &c., traduite en Arménien et augmentée par le P. Aristarkes, Mekhitariste de Venise.

8*vo*., Venice, 1881

———————————————— Les Comtes du Carpas. (Extrait de la Bibliothèque de l'école des Chartes, t. xii.)

8*vo*., Paris, 1882

———————————————— Histoire des Archevêques Latins de l'île de Chypre. (Société de l'Orient Latin, t. ii., 1882, pp. 207–328.)

8*vo*., Génes, 1882

———————————————— Documents nouveaux servant de preuves à l'histoire de l'île de Chypre sous le règne des princes de la maison de Lusignan (Collection des documents inédits, t. ix.) 4*to*., Paris, 1882

———————————————— Texte official de l'allocution addressée par les Barons de Chypre au roi Henri II. de Lusignan pour lui notifier sa déchéance. (Revue des Questions historiques, t. xlv.) 8*vo*., Paris, 1888

———————————————— Découvertes récentes en **Chypre**. (ibidem.) 1888

———————————————— Découverte des tombeaux d'un Prince de Lusignan. et du Maréchal Adam d'Antioche. (Note extraite de la Revue illustrée de la Terre Sainte.)

8*vo*., Paris, 1889

———————————————— Registre des lettres du Roi de Chypre. (Bibl. de l'école des Chartes, t. LV., p. 235.)

8*vo*., Paris, 1894

MONTASIO, ENR. Caterina Cornaro e i suoi amori. (Articolo nel Vaglio, 7 Feb) 8*vo*., Venice, 1846

LONGO, FR. Successo della guerra fatta con Selim Sultan e giustificazione della pace con lui conchiusa 1569–1573. (App. dell'Archivio Storico Ital., No. 17.) 8*vo*., Firenze, 1847

MARGARITES, D. Περὶ Κύπρου διατριβὴ περιέχουσα διαφόρους πληροφορίας καταστατικὰς, γεωγραφικὰς, κτλ. Athens, 1849

SPERDUTI, GAB. Iolanda di Cipro, tragedia in cinque atti. 12*mo*., Milano, 1847

CHESNEY, LT.-COL. R.A. Expedition for the Survey of the Euphrates and Tigris. *2 vols., 8vo.*, London, 1850

NOTIZIE Intorno a Catarina Corner, Regina di Cipro. (Nozze Rota-Luccheschi.) *8vo.*, Venice, 1851

KELLY, ——. Macariæ Excidium, or the Destruction of Cyprus. Irish and English.
(Irish Archæological and Celtic Society, No. 13. *Really a secret history of the war of the Revolution in Ireland* 1688–91 *written under the title of* Macariæ Excidium, &c.) *4to.*, Dublin, 1853

LACROIX, L. Les Iles de la Grèce. *8vo.*, Paris, 1853

ESCHAVANNES, E. D' Notice historique sur la maison de Lusignan. *8vo.*, Paris, 1853

MARMONT, A. F. L., Duc de Ragusa. The present State of the Turkish Empire.
(Translated, with notes, by F. Smith.) London, 1854

SMYTH, REAR-ADM. W. The Mediterranean. A Memoir. *8vo.*, London, 1854

SAKELLARIOS, ATH. Τὰ Κυπριακά. *8vo*, Athens, vol. i., 1855, & iii., 1868

———————————— Τὰ Κυπριακά.
Vol. i. Γεωγραφία, Ἱστορία, δημόσιος καὶ ἰδιωτικὸς βίος. *Royal 8vo.*, Athens, 1890

Vol. ii. Ἡ ἐν Κύπρῳ γλῶσσα. *Royal, 8vo.*, Athens, 1891

GAUDRY, ALBERT Recherches Scientifiques en Orient. *Royal 8vo.*, Paris, 1855

———————————— L'île de Chypre. Souvenirs d'une mission scientifique. *8vo.*, *pp.* 28, Paris, 1861

——— ————————— Géologie de l'île de Chypre. *4to.*, Paris, 1862

———————————— do. do. (Translated by F. Maurice, Capt. R.A.) *Fol.*, London, 1878

REINHARDT De rebus Cypriis. *4to.*, Frankfort, 1857

COXE, H. O. Report to Her Majesty's Government on the Greek MSS yet remaining in Libraries of the Levant.
(Cyprus, pp. 17–19 and 69, 70.) *8vo.*, London, 1858

ANON. The siege of Famagosta, or, the Soldier Martyr. *12mo.*, London, 1858

CAUMONT, NOMPAR, SEIGNEUR DE Voyaige d'oultremer en Jhérusalem (1418) publié par le Marquis de La Grange. *8vo.*, Paris, 1858

LANGLOIS, VICTOR Documents pour servir à l'histoire des Lusignans de la petite Armènic 1342–1394. *8vo.*, Paris, 1859

VOGÜÉ, MARQUIS MELCHIOR DE Coup d'œil sur les monuments de Chypre et de Rhodes.
(Les Eglises de la Terre Sainte, pp. 376--389.) *4to.*, Paris, 1860

HEUZEY LÉON Les figurines antiques de terre cuite du Musée du Louvre.· *Fol.*, Paris, 1860 & 1883

———————— *Id.* (Cyprus. pp. 113-203.) 16*mo.*, Paris, 1891

—————————— Vases à Figurines de Chypre. (Gazette arch.. 1889.)
4to., Paris, 1889

BRENTANO, CLEMENT Vie de N.-S. Jésus Christ d'après les visions d'Anne Catherine Emmerich, traduite par M. l'abbè de Cazalès.
(*Les visions rapportent un séjour de N.-S. en Chypre qui fut d'environ six semaines.*) Paris, 1861

KOTSCHY, T. Reise nach Cypern und Klein Asien. 1859.
(An article in Petermann's Mittheilungen, viii.) *4to.*, Gotha, 1862

CANALE, M. G. De Mas Latrie's History reviewed. (Archivio Storico It. n.s., xvi., p. 2) *8vo.*, Firenze, 1862

VOGÜÉ, M. Fouilles de Chypre et de Syrie, extraits de lettres à M.M. Renan et A. de Longperier. (Revue Arch. N.S., No. VI., p. 244.)
8vo., Paris, 1862

STARK, K. B. Der Cyprische Torso d. Berliner Museums (No. 796) Gr. Grabreliefs. Ein archæol. Räthsel. *4to.*, Berlin, 1863

ANON. Κύπρος καὶ Πάφος. (Πανδώρα, xv.; 148, 171.)
4to., Athens, 1864

GRAVIER, CH. DU ROYAL, SR. DU Voyage de Jèrusalem et autres lieux Saincts effectué et décrit en 1644. Ed. par Bonnemesse de Saint Denis. *8vo.*, Paris, 1864

SELANIKLI MUSTAFA Tarikh. (Conquest of Cyprus, pp. 100–102.)
8vo., Constantinople (A.H. 1281), 1864

ANON. Ἀγγεῖον Ἀμαθοῦντος (Πανδώρα, xv., 40.)
4to., Athens, 1865

UNGER, FRANZ, und T. KOTSCHY Die Insel Cypern.
8vo., Wien, 1865

———————————————————— Die Insel Cypern einst und jetzt. *8vo.*, Wien, 1866

CONSTITUTIO CYPRIA. (Patrol. Gr. ed Migne, t. 140, col. 1544.)
8vo., Paris, 1865

BULLA AD EPISCOPOS GRÆCOS, ETC. In Insula Cypro constitutos. (Patrol. Gr. ed Migne, t. 140, col. 1561.) *8vo.*, Paris, 1865

SCHARFE, J. De Evagoræ Salaminiorum reguli vita.
Munster, 1866

PECHEVI IBRAHIM PASHA Tarikh. (Conquest of Cyprus, I., 486–491.) *8vo.*, Constantinople (A.H. 1283), 1866

PADOVAN, VINCENZO Il Martire di Famagosta, Carme.
(Nozze Squeraroli—Sartori.) *8vo.*, Venice, 1866

FOURNIER, EUG. Sur les noms anciens du Cyprés: recherches étymologiques. (Actes du Congrès internat. de Botanique, Paris, Aout, 1867.) *8vo.*, Paris, 1867

ANON.   Κύπρου ἀνάγλυφον.   (Νέα Πανδώρα, xviii., 458.)
4to., Athens, 1867

SAMAGEUILT, J. F.·   De la communauté d'origine des Lusignan d'Agenais et des Lusignan du Poitou : Mémoire.
8ro., Villeneuve sur Lot, 1868

BOSQ, DUBERNET DE   Complément à la notice historique sur les Lusignan d'Agenais et du Poitou.   8ro., Agen, 1868

VIDAL LABLACHE   Statuette Cypriote du Musée d'Athenes.   (Revue arch. Nouv. Sèrie. Vol. XIX., p. 341.)   8ro., Paris, 1869

COLUCCI, CAV. RICCARDO   La Viticoltura e Vinificazione nella provincia di Limassol.
(Bolletino Consolare, vol. v. parte ii. fasc. iii.)   8ro., Rome, 1869

MYRIANTHEUS, HIERON.   Περὶ τῶν 'Αρχαίων Κυπρίων.
8vo., Athens, 1868 ; 2nd ed., 1869

DU CANGE (ed. E. G. REY)   Les familles d'Outre-mer.
Les rois de Chypre, pp, 49–101 ; Les grands officiers, pp. 663–693 ; Les archevêques et évêques, pp. 843–868.)   4to., Paris, 1869

SIBITANIDES, G. N.   'Η Κύπρος καὶ οἱ Ναῖται—Δρᾶμα.
8vo., Alexandria, 1869

HERQUET, KARL   Charlotta von Lusignan und Caterina Cornaro, Könniginnen von Cypern.   8ro., Regensburg, 1870

————————— Cyprische Königsgestalten des Hauses Lusignan.
8vo., Halle, 1881

CANNONERO, R.   Storia dell' Isola di Cipro : Parte prima.
8vo., pp. 116, Imola, 1870

CESNOLA, LOUIS P. D.   Antiquités Cypriotes provenant des fouilles faites en 1868 par M. di Cesnola.   La vente aux enchères publiques aura lieu les 25 et 26 mars, 1870, 387 lots.   Royal 8ro. Paris, 1870

————————————— The antiquities of Cyprus, discovered principally on the sites of the ancient Golgoi and Idalium......photographed by Stephen Thompson, with an introduction by Sidney Colvin.
Fol., London, 1873

————————— Le ultime scoperte nell' isola di Cipro.
(Estr. dagli atti della R. Acc. delle Scienze di Torino, vol xi.)
8vo., Torino., 1876

————————— Cyprus : its ancient Cities, Tombs and Temples.   8vo.. London, 1877

————————— Cyprus : its ancient Art and History.   Four lectures.
(New York Tribune, extra No. 47, Nov. 27, 1878.) Fol., New York, 1878

————————— Cypern .... autorisirte deutsche Bearheitung, von Ludwig Stern   Royal 8vo., Jena, 1879 and 1881

————————— A descriptive Atlas of the Cesnola Collection of Cypriote Antiquities in the Metropolitan Museum of Art, New York.
3 vols., fol., Boston, 1884–6

STARK, K. B.　Leierspielende Frau (Sappho?) Statue aus Cypern. (Arch. Zeit. XXVIII., pp. 67-76.)　　　　*4to.*, Berlin, 1871

REY, E. G.　Etude sur les monuments de l'architecture militaire des Croisés en Syrie et dans l'île de Chypre.　　　　*4to.*, Paris, 1871

SATHAS, C. N.　Bibliotheca Græca Medii Œvi.
　　　　　　　　6 *vols.*, *8vo.*, Venice and Paris, 1872-77
(Vol. ii. contains χρονογράφοι τοῦ βασιλείου τῆς Κύπρου. Νεόφυτος Ἐγκλειστος, Λεόντιος Μαχαιρᾶς, Γεώργιος Βουστρώνιος, Νεόφυτος Ῥοδινός, Ἀνέκδοτα νομίσματα ὑπὸ Π. Λάμπρου.
Vol. vi., pp. 1-497 Ἀσίζαι τοῦ βασιλεῖυ των Ἱεροσολύμων κ̃ τῆς Κύπρου. pp. 499-585 Ἑλληνικοὶ νόμοι ἰσχύοντες ἐν Κύπρῳ ἐπὶ τῆς Φραγκοκρατίας.)

FRIEDRICHS, C.　Kunst und Leben, Reisebriefe aus Griechenland, dem Orient und Italien.　　　　*8vo.*, Düsseldorf, 1872

AUSTRIA, ARCHDUKE LOUIS SALVATOR OF　Levkosia, die Hauptstadt von Cypern.　　　　*4to.*, Prag, 1873

———————————————————————————— Levkosia. The Capital of Cyprus.　　　　*4to.*, London, 1881

DOELL, JOHANNES　Die Sammlung Cesnola.
　(Mémoires de l'Académie de S. Pétersbourg, vii. sér. xix., no. 4, 1873.)

COLLECTION　importante de vases antiques, bijoux, terres cuites, provenant de fouilles faites dans l'île de Chypre par M. Pierides.　261 lots.　　　　*8vo.*, Paris, 1873

GAMS, PIUS B.　Series episcoporum Ecclesiæ Catholicæ. (Bishops of Paphos, Famagusta and Neapolis, pp. 438, 9.)
　　　　　　　　4to., Ratisbon, 1873-86

SHEMS EL DIN DIMISHQI (1256-1327) Manuel de la Cosmographie, traduit par A. F. Mehren.　　　　*8vo.*. Copenhagen, 1874

LOUKA, G.　Φιλολογικαὶ ἐπισκέψεις.　*Vol. I.*, *8vo.*, Athens, 1874

TAFUR PERO　Andanças e Viajes, 1435-39. (Ginesta.　Collecion de libros espanoles raros o curiosos, VIII., & IX.)
　　　　　　　2 *vols.*, Madrid, 12*mo.*, 1874

CAMMEN, E. P. VAN DER　Etude sur l'île de Chypre.
　　　　　　　　8vo., Bruxelles, 1874

D'ESTOURNELLE DE CONSTANT　L' Ile de Chypre d'après M. Loukas. (Annuaire de l'ass. pour l'encouragement des études grecques en France.)　　　　*8vo.*, Paris, 1875

SALOUMIDES, S. M.　Οἱ ἀνακαλυφθέντες Θησαυροὶ τῶν ἀρχαιοτήτων τῆς Κύπρου. Δημοσιευθέντες διὰ τῆς ἐφημερίδος Ἀνατολῆς, ἔπειτα διὰ τῆς ἐφ. τῶν φιλομαθῶν, νῦν δὲ διὰ τοῦ παρόντος φυλλαδίου μετά τινων συμπληρώσεων καὶ ἐπιδιορθώσεων.　pp. 23.
　　　　　　　　8vo., Athens, 1875

UNGER, ROBERT　Paralipomena rerum Cypriacarum.
　　　　　　　　4to., Halle, 1875

SEIFF, JULIUS　Skizze einer Reise durch die Insel Cypern.
　　　　　　　　8vo., Dresden, 1874

SEIFF, JULIUS   Reisen in der asiatischen Türkei.
8vo., Leipzig, 1875

GEORGIOU, PHILIPPOS Εἰδήσεις ἱστορικαὶ περὶ τῆς ἐκκλησίας τῆς Κύπρου.   *8ro.*, Athens, 1875

PODACATARO, ALESS. Relatione de' successi di Famagosta dell' anno 1571 ora per la prima volta publicata. (*Nozze Bonomi -Bragadin.*)
8ro., Venezia, 1876

HELLE VON SAMO, A. RITTER ZU Das Vilayet der Inseln d. Weissen Meeres, das privilegirte Beylik Samos, und das selbständige Mutessariflik Cypern.   *Royal 8ro.*, Vienna, 1876

—————————————— Translated in the Geographical Magazine, July and August, 1878.

VONDIZIANO, C. A. Ἱστορία τῆς νήσου Κύπρου.
(From the French of L. Lacroix.) *8ro.*, Athens, 1877

SANDWITH, T. B. Styles of Pottery found in ancient Tombs in Cyprus. (Archæologia, XLV., pp. 127–142.)   *4to.*, London, 1877

ORCET, G. D' Chypre, une des guérites de l'isthme de Suez.
(Revue Britannique, t. v., pp. 77–104.) 1877

MACHAUT, GUILLAUME DE La Prise d'Alexandrie, ou chronique du Roi Pierre de Lusignan, ed. L. de Mas Latrie.
8ro., Geneva, 1877

SAYCE, A. H. The Babylonian Cylinders found by General di Cesnola in the Treasury of the Temple of Kurium.
(Tr. S. B. A., v. 2, pp. 441–444.)   *8vo.*, London, 1877

HALL, I. H. On two terra cotta lamps found in Cyprus. (Proc. Am. Or. Soc. vi., vii.)   *8ro.*, New York, 1877

SCHLUMBERGER, G. Les Principautés franques du Levant.
8ro., Paris, 1877

————————————————— Sigillographie byzantine...des ducs et capetans de Chypre.   *8ro.*, Genoa, 1883

NEUBAUER, R. Der angebliche Aphrodite–tempel zu Golgoi, und die daselbst gefundenen Inschriften in Kyprischer Schift.
(*Commentationes philologæ in honorem Theod. Mommseni*, pp. 673–93.)
4to., Berlin, 1877

LENORMANT, FR. (E. DE CHANOT) Statues iconiques du temple d'Athiénou. (Gaz. arch. IV., p. 192.)   *4to.*, Paris, 1878

PERROT, G. L' Ile de Chypre ; son rôle dans l'histoire. (Revue des deux mondes, 1 Dec., 1878, 15 Fev., 15 Mai, 1879.)
Royal 8ro., Paris, 1878-79

SCHRÖDER, PAUL Meine zweite Reise auf Cypern im Frühjahr 1873. (Globus, pp. 135–186.)   *8vo.*, Brunswick, 1878

LÖHER, FR. VON Kaiser Friedrich II. Kampf um Cypern.
(Abhandl. der K. bayer. Acad. der Wissenschaften, III. Cl. XIV, Bd. II. Abth.)   *4to.*, München, 1878

LÖHER, FR. VON   Cypern. Reiseberichte über Natur und Land-schaft, Volk und Geschichte.   *8vo.*, Stuttgart, 1878
  3rd ed., 1879

———————————— Cyprus. Historical and Descriptive.

(From Von Löher, by Mrs. A. B. Joyner.) *12mo.*, London, 1878
———————————— Cypern in der Geschichte.

8vo., Berlin, 1878

LANG, R. H.   Narrative of Excavations in a Temple at Dali (Idalion) in Cyprus.

(Tr. R. Soc. of Literature, 2nd series, Vol. xi. Part I.)

8vo., London, 1878

———————— Cyprus.   Its History, its present resources and future prospects.   *8vo.*, London, 1878
———————— Chypre.   Traduit de l'anglais par V. Dave.

18mo., Paris, 1879

———————— Handbook to Cyprus, and Catalogue of the Exhibits. (Colonial and Indian Exhibition.)   *12mo.*, London, 1886

———————— Report upon the Results of the Cyprus Representation at the Colonial and Indian Exhibition of 1886.

12mo., London, 1886

ANON.   Gooin to Cyprus : by Ab-o'th'yate.

8vo., Manchester, 1878 and 1879

——— Cyprus, Syria, and Palestine, the future emporium of British trade in Asia.   By a Consul-General.   *8vo.*, London, 1878

——— Aperçu rapide sur l'ile de Chypre.   Par un Membre de la Société de Géographie   *8vo.*, Montpellier, 1878

——— Jacques Roux de Lusignan.   La vérité sur la famille des Lusignan du Levant.   *8vo.*, Paris,

——— The occupation of Cyprus : immediate and probable effects.   By an Ex-Consul-General.   *16mo.*, London, 1878

——— (M. J.) Cyprus and Asiatic Turkey.   A handy general de-scription.   *8vo.*, London, 1878

ROSTOVITZ, A.   Cyprus : special report by the representative of MM. Thos. Cook and Son.   *8vo.*, s.l., 1878

GLOVER, R.   Cyprus : the Christian history of our new Colonial gem.

8vo., London, 1878

GAMMON, F. T.   Cyprus : its history and prospects.

8vo.. London, 1878

CLARKE, E.   Cyprus, past and present.   *8vo.*, London, 1878

MAGEN, EUGÈNE   Le vase d'Amathonte.   Relation de son transport en France.   *8vo.*, Agen, 1867 and 1878

STUBBS, W. BISHOP OF OXFORD.   The medieval Kingdoms of Cyprus and Armenia.   Two Lectures.   *4to.*, Oxford, 1878

COLLEN, CAPT. E. H. H. A Report on Cyprus, 1845-1877.
(Intelligence Branch, Q. M. G. Dept.) 8vo., London, 1878

SAVILLE, CAPT. A. R. Cyprus.
(Intelligence Branch, Q. M. G. Dept.) 8vo., London, 1878

ANON. Cyprus : its value and importance to England.
8vo., London, 1878

DAVIDSON, J. T. Cyprus. its place in Bible History.
16mo., London, 1878

THOMAS, G. M. Über die älteren Besitzungen der Venezianer auf Cypern. (Sitzungsberichte d. K. B. Acad. der Wissenschaften.)
8vo., München, 1878

FISHER, F. H. Cyprus : our new Colony   8vo., London, 1878

HARRIS, C. D. Cyprus : its Past, Present and Future.
8vo., London, 1878

LAKE, J. J. Ceded Cyprus.   8vo., London, 1878

ROBINSON, PHIL. Cyprus.   8vo., London, 1878

SANDFORD, C. W., Bishop of Gibraltar. England's Rule in Cyprus.
A Sermon.   8vo., Oxford, 1878

——————————— Our Church in Cyprus. A Sermon.
8vo., Oxford, 1886

——————————— Ἡ ἐν Κύπρῳ ἐκκλησία μας.
(Translated into Modern Greek by C. D. Cobham.) 8vo., Larnaca, 1886

FARLEY, J. L. Egypt, Cyprus and Asiatic Turkey.
8vo., London, 1878

TAYLOR, BAYARD Ephesus, Cyprus and Mycenæ.
(N. American Review, Jan., Feb., no. 260, pp. 111.)   1878

FROEHNER, W. Catalogue illustré de la collection de M. Albert Barre ......Poterie et Verres Cypriotes.   4to., Paris, April, 1878

SASSENAY, MARQUIS DE Chypre, histoire et géographie.
8vo., Paris, 1878

CHEON, . DE L'ile de Chypre et la République Française au congrés de Berlin.   8vo., Paris, 1878

AUBERIVERE, H. F. P. DE L' Aperçu rapide sur l'île de Chypre.
8vo., Montpellier, 1878

GORRESIO, G. Nota sulla Croce gammata dei monumenti recentemente scoperti nell' isola di Cipro.   4to. (pp. 4), Turin, 1878

RAVENSTEIN, E. G. Cyprus ; its resources and capabilities, with hints for tourists.   8vo., London, 1878

BAKER, SIR S. Cyprus as I saw it in 1879.   8vo., London, 1879
——————— Cypern. Aus den Englischen, von Richard Oberländer.
8vo., Leipzig, 1880

CASSEL, P. Cypern, Eine Abhandlung.   8vo., Berlin, 1879

SORLIN-DORIGNY Statue colossale découverte à Amathonte. (Gaz. arch., p. 230.) *4to.*, Paris, 1879

MÜLLER, AUGUST Zur Ornithologie der Insel Cypern. (Journal F. O., pp. 385–393.) *8vo.*, Leipzig, 1879

BRASSEY, TH. Recent letters and speeches. (The future of Cyprus. Condition of Cyprus, &c.) *8vo.*, London, 1879

POTTIER, EDM. Description de quelques monuments figurès de l'ile de Chypre. (Acad. des Iuser. et B. L. Comptes rendus, 1878, p. 197. Bulletin de correspondance hellénique, Mai, 1897.) *4to.*, Paris, 1879

KITCHENER, H. H. Notes on Cyprus. (Blackwood's Magazine, Aug., 1879.) *8ro.*, Edinburg, 1879

PESARO, ELIE DE Voyage de Venise à Famagouste en 1563. (Texte Hebreu publié par B. Goldberg et M. Adelman dans *La Vie Éternelle.*) *8vo.*, Vienna, 1878

——————————— Voyage ethnographique de Venise à Chypre. Ed. Moise Schwab. (Revue de Géographie, Sept., 1879.) *8ro.*, Paris, 1879

LAURIA Studj sull' Isola di Cipro. 1879

ANON. Geography of Cyprus. *16mo.*, Leicester, 1879

HEYD, W. Geschichte des Levantehandels im mittelalter. *8ro.*, 2 *vols.*, Stuttgart, 1879

——————— Histoire du Commerce du Levant au moyen âge, trad. Furcy-Reynaud. 2 *vols.*, *8ro.*, Leipzig, 1885, 1886

ANON. The Secret of Cyprus and our Eastern Protectorate : By Theta. *8ro.*, Haverfordwest, 1879

SCHINAS, G. C. AND GALIZIA, E. L. Island of Cyprus. Report to the Governor of Malta. *Fol.*, Malta, 1879

SCHNEIDER, KARL Cypern unter den Engländern. *8vo.*, Köln, 1879

CRENNEVILLE, VICTOR F. DE Die Insel Cypern. *8ro.*, Wien, 1879

THOMSON, J. Through Cyprus with the camera in the autumn of 1878 2 *vols.*, *4to.*, London, 1879

GHINZONI, P. Gal. M. Sforza e il regno di Cipro, 1473-74. *4to.*, Milano, 1879

RICHTER, M. O. Ein Heiligthum der Syrischen Astarte. (Ausland, p. 970.) 1879

——————— Von den neusten Ausgrabungen in der Cyprischen Salamis. (Mitth. des D. Arch. Inst., vol. vi.) *8vo.*, 1881

——————— Die Cyprische Biene und deren Zucht auf Cypern. (Der Bienenvater aus Böhmen, Oct.—Dec., 1882, Jan.—Feb., 1883.) *8vo.*, Marienbad, 1882-3

——————— Ein altes Bauwerk bei Larnaca. (Abdruck aus der Arch. Zeitung.) *4to.*, Berlin, 1882

RICHTER, M. O. A Pre-historic Building at Salamis. (Translated, with note, by C. D. Cobham, Journal of Hellenic Studies, vol. iv., April, 1883.) *8vo.*, London, 1883

———————— On a Phoenician Vase found in Cyprus.
(J. of H. S. vol. v.) *8vo.*, London, 1884

———————— Heiligthum des Apollon bei Voni.
(Mitth. des D. Arch. Inst., vol. ix.) *8vo.*, Athens, 1884

———————— Das Museum und die Ausgrabungen auf Cypern seit 1878.
(Repertorium für Kunstwissenschaft, ix. Band.) *8vo.*, Stuttgart, 1886

———————— Cyprische Vasc aus Athienu.
(Jahrbuch der K. Deutschen Archäologischen Institnts, Band i.)
4to., Berlin, 1886

———————— Cyperus Cultur im Alterthume.
(Mitt. der anthropol, Ges. in Wien, Band xx., ss. 90–95.)
4to., Vienna, 1890

———————— Die antiken Cultusstätten auf Kypros.
4to., Berlin, 1891

———————— Ancient places of worship in Kypros catalogued and described. *4to.*, Berlin, 1891

———————— Kypros, the Bible and Homer.
2 vols., royal *4to.*, London, 1893

———————— Kypros, die Bibel und Homer.
2 vols., royal *4to.*, Berlin, 1893

———————— Parallelen und Gebräuche der alten und der jetzigen Bevolkerung von Cypern.
(Ges. Anthr. Ethu. und Urgesch. s. 34–43.) *8vo.*, Berlin, 1891

———————— Græco-Phoenician Architecture in Cyprus, with special reference to the origin and development of the Ionic Volute. (I. R. I. Br. Architects, IIIrd Series, Vol. III., No. 4, pp. 109–134.)
4to., London, 1895

———————— and **MYRES, J. L.** Catalogue of the Cyprus Museum. (See Myres, J. L., 1899.)

BROWN, S. Three months in Cyprus during the winter of 1878–9. Paper read at meeting of British Association at Sheffield, Aug. 25, 1879.
12mo., London, 1879

———————— The Locust War in Cyprus. *12mo.*, London, 1886

ANON. Del successo di Famagosta. Diario d'un Contemporaneo.
(Nozze Gozzi-Guaita.) *8vo.*, Venezia, 1879

MAGNI, RENATO Casa di Savoja e l'isola di Cipro, Appunti storici.
(Bollettino Consolare, vol. xv., fasc. vii.) *8vo.*, Roma, 1879

DIXON, W. HEPWORTH British Cyprus. *8vo.*, London, 1879

MARTIN, ADM. SIR W. F. Cyprus as a Naval Station and a Place of Arms. *8vo.*, London, 1879

OLIVIER, G. P. TESTAFFERATA and E. L. GALIZIA Report
on Lands in Cyprus for a Maltese Settlement. *Fol.*, London, 1880

STEVENSON, MRS. E. S. Our Home in Cyprus.
         8vo., London, 1880

LUIGGI, LUIGI L'Isola di Cipro.   *8vo.*, Roma, 1880

CAZENOVE, RAOUL DE Notes sur l'isle de Chypre. Souvenirs et
impressions d'un voyage à travers les livres. *8vo.*, Lyon, 1880

BRASSEY, ANNIE, LADY Sunshine and Storm in the East: or cruises
to Cyprus and Constantinople. *8vo. and crown 8vo.*, London, 1880

TWISS, SIR TRAVERS Cyprus, its mediaeval jurisprudence and
modern legislation.
(Law Magazine and Review, No. 236, May, 1880.) *8vo.*, London, 1880

BUCHAN, A. The Climate of Cyprus from observations made by T. B.
Sandwith, 1866-1870.
    (Journ. Scottish Meteor. Soc. N.S.V. 189-193.) 1880

POTTIER, EDM. Les hypogées doriques de Nea-Paphos dans l' Ile de
Chypre.
    (Bulletin de Corr. Hell. iv., pp. 497-505.) *4to.*, Paris, 1880

————————— Catalogue des Vases antiques de terre cuite. Musée
du Louvre. (Chypre, pp. 82-118.)   *16mo.*, Paris, 1896

————————— Vases antiques du Louvre. (Chypre. pp. 5-10.)
            4to., Paris, 1897

DOZON, A. Commerce de l'ile de Chypre. (Bull. Cons. Français,
No 6.)   *8vo.*, Paris, 1880

ANGLURE, ORIENT D'OGER, SEIGNEUR D' Le Saint voyage de
Jérusalem. Ed. par Fr. Bonnardot et Aug. Longnon. (Soc. des
anciens Textes.)   *8vo.*, Paris, 1880

KELLER, JAKOB Die Cyprischen Alterthums-funde. (Samml. f. gem.
Wissenschaftlicher Vorträge, No. 363.) *8vo.*, Berlin, 1881

BENT, J. TH. A pilgrimage to Cyprus in 1395-96. (Fraser's Magazine,
pp. 818-21, June, 1881.)   *8vo.*, London, 1881

MADDALENA, G. Cenni sull' isola di Cipro nel 1880. (Boll. Cons.
Maggio, 1881.)   *8vo.*, Roma, 1881

LÖHER, FRANZ VON Die Ausgrabungen auf Cypern. (Ill. Deutsche
Monatshefte, 655-664.)   *8vo.*, Berlin, 1881

CESNOLA, ALEX. P. DI Lawrence-Cesnola collection. Cyprus antiquities excavated by A. P. di Cesnola, 1876-79. *4to.*, London, 1881

————————— Salaminia. The History, Treasures and
Antiquities of Salamis, in the Isle of Cyprus. *8vo.*, London, 1882

————————— On specimens of ancient goldsmiths' art
found in Cyprus. (Br. Arch. J., June 30, 1883, Vol. XXXIX., Part II.)
          8vo., London, 1883

————————— Oro e vetri antichi di Cypro scavati negli
anni 1876 and 1879.   *8vo.*, Torino, 1884

ČESNÖLA, ALEX. P. DI Salamina. Storia, tesori e antichità.
4to., Torino, 1887

GAMBA, A. Nota relativa ad alcuni preziosi oggetti tratti da scavi nell' isola di Cipro del Cav. A. P. di Cesnola, 8vo., Torino, 1881

MACHÆRA, LEONTIOU Χρονικὸν Κύπρου.
(Texte Gree et traduction Française ; ed. C. Sathas et E. Muller.)
2 vols., royal 8vo., Paris, 1882

CLARKE, HYDE The early history of the Mediterranean populations in their migrations and settlements. 8vo., London, 1882

MICHAELIDES, BASIL 'Η ἀσθενὴς Λύρα. Λυρικὰ Ποιημάτια.
8vo., Limassol, 1882

PETRIDES, I. Διομήδης. Δρᾶμα εἰς πράξεις πέντε.
8vo., Limassol, 1882

REINSCH, P. F. On a new mineral found in the Island of Cyprus.
(Proc. Royal Soc. xxxiii., 119-121.) 4to., London, 1882

SCHRADER, EB. Die Sargons stele des Berliner Museums.
8vo., Berlin, 1882

———————— Zur Geographie des Assyrischen Reichs. (Kition
ǀ p. 337-344. 8vo., Berlin, 1890

COLONNA CECCALDI, GEO. Monuments antiques de Chypre, de Syrie et d'Egypte. 8vo., Paris, 1882

SINTENIS, PAUL Eine Reiseskizze über Cypern and seine Flora.
(Oest. bot. Zeitschrift,' 1881, pp. 225-32.) 8vo., Vienna, 1882

I'ANSON, E. and S. VACHER Mediæval and other Buildings in the Isle of Cyprus. 4to., London, 1883

ACTES passés à Famagosta de 1292 à 1301 par devant le notaire génois Lambert de Sambucato, publiés par le Chev. Cornelio de Simoni.
Gènes, 1883

FONTANA, E. Περὶ χολέρας.
('Εκδοθεῖσα δαπάναις τοῦ Δημαρχείου Λευκωσίας.) 8vo , Nicosia, 1883

THEOCHARIDES, THEM. Δύο σκηναὶ τῆς Κυπριακῆς 'Ιστορίας.
2 parts, 12mo., Larnaca, 1884

———————— Συλλογὴ ποιημάτων.
12mo., Nicosia, 1886

———————— 'Η ἀνέγερσις τοῦ Λαζάρου, Ποίημα.
8vo., Larnaca, 1888

HERACLIDES, TH. Τραγούδιον τῆς Θεονίτσας.
12mo., ἐν Κύπρῳ, 1884 and 1889

ABD EL RAHMAN, IBN ABI BAKR Unternehmungen der Mamluken gegen Cypern und Rhodus in den Jahren 1423-44 nach Christo, Auszug aus des Gelâl-ed-Din es-Siyuti Geschichte des Sultans el-Melek el Aschraf Qait bâj. Arabisch und Deutsch mit Anmerkungen von A. Wahrmund. 8vo., Vienna, 1884

ENMANN, A.　Kritische Versuche zur ältesten griechischen Geschichte.
I. Kypros. und der Ursprung des Aphrodite Kultus.
Royal 4to., Petersburg, 1887

COBHAM, C. D.　An attempt at a Bibliography of Cyprus.
(Privately printed.)　12mo., Nicosia, 1886, 1889, 1894 and 1900

———————————— Ilmu Hal.　A manual of the Doctrine and Practice of
Islam.　Translated from the Turkish.
(Privately printed.)　*8vo.*. Nicosia, 1886

———————————— Excerpta Cypria, translated and transcribed by.
4to., Nicosia, 1895

———————————— The story of Umm Haram.　Turkish and English.
(Journal of the R. As. Soc., January, 1897.)　*8vo.*, London, 1897

———————————— Laws and Regulations affecting Waqf property.
8vo., Nicosia, 1899

——————————— *See Graziani, 1624, Mariti, 1769, Sandford, 1886.*

ROSSBACH, O.　Zum Thongefäss von Athienu.
(Mitt. d. deutschen Arch. Inst. Athen, Abth xi.)　*8vo.*, Athens, 1886

UNDSET, INGVALD　Ein Kyprisches Eisenschwert.
8vo., Christiania, 1886

SCHOTTMUELLER, K.　Processus Cypriensis.
(Der Untergang des Templer-Ordens, Bd. ii., p. 141.) *8vo.*, Berlin, 1887

SMITH, AGNES　Through Cyprus.
8vo., London, 1887

GIBELLI, FED. DE　Corona di fiori poetici.
4to., Nicosia, 1887

PAISIOS, L.　Ἐγχειρίδιον τοπογραφίας καὶ ἱστορίας τῆς νήσου Κύπρου.
12mo., Varosha, 1887

MATHAIOU, BASILEIOS　Βιογραφία, Θάνατος καὶ Κηδεία τοῦ Μητρο-
πολίτου Κιτίου Κυπριανοῦ.
4to., Alexandria, 1887

MICHAELIDES, PERICLES　Στοιχειώδης πολιτικὴ γεωγραφία τῆς νήσου
Κύπρου.
12mo., Tulcha, 1887

GESTES DES CHIPROIS.　Recueil de chroniques françaises écrites en
Orient aux xiiie. et xive. siécles (Philippe de Navarre et Gérard de
Monréal) publié pour la première fois pour la Société de l'orient Latin.
Royal 8vo., Geneva, 1887

REY, E.　L'Ordre du Temple en Syrie et à Chypre.　Les Templiers en
Terre Sainte.
8vo. Arcis-Sur-Aube, 1888

CONSTANTINIDES, TH. PH.　Ὁ Κουτσοὺκ Μεχμὲτ ἤ τὸ 1821 ἐν
Κύπρῳ.　Δρᾶμα ἱστορικὸ
8vo., Alexandria, 1888

ZIMMERER, H.　Die Englische Generalstabskarte von Cypern.
8vo., Munich. 1888

GUILLEMARD, Dr. H. H.　Ornithological Tour in Cyprus.
(Ibis, 1888, pp. 94-124.)　*8vo.*, London, 1888

——————————————— Cyprus and its birds in 1888.
(Ibis, 1888, p. 206.)　*8vo.*, London, 1889

LILFORD, T. L. LORD   A History of the Birds of Cyprus.
(Ibis, 1888, p. 305.) 8*vo.*, London, 1889

KEPIADES, G. I.   Ἀπομνημονεύματα τῶν κατὰ τὸ 1821 ἐν τῇ νήσῳ Κύπρῳ τραγικῶν σκηνῶν.   12*mo.*, Alexandria, 1888

HERMANN, PAUL   Das Gräberfeld von Marion auf Cypern.
(Winckelmann's Programm, 1888.) *4to.*, Berlin, 1888

GRAVIERE, V. AM. EDMOND DE LA   La Guerre de Chypre et la bataille de Lepaute. Ouvrage accompagné de quatorze cartes et plans.
2 *vols.*, 8*vo.*, Paris, 1888

MALLOCK, W. H.   Scenes in Cyprus.
(Scribner, vol. iv., no. 21.) 8*vo.*, New York, 1888

———————— In an Enchanted Island ; or a Winter's Retreat in
Cyprus.   *Dy.* 8*vo.*, London, 1889 and 1892

GARDNER, E. A. HOGARTH, D. G. · JAMES, M. R. ELSEY SMITH, R.   Excavations in Cyprus, 1887–8. Paphos, Leontari, Amargetti. (Journal of Hellenic Studies, vol. ix., no. 2.)
Royal 8*vo.*, London, 1888

DESIMONI, C.   Actes passées à Famagouste de 1299 à 1301 par devant le notaire Génois Lamberto di Sambuceto.
(Archives de l'Orient Latin, II. Documents, pp. 1–120.)
Royal 8*vo.*, Paris, 1884

———————— Notes et observations sur les actes du notaire Génois Lamberto di Sambuceto. (Revue de l'Orient Latin, 1894. No. 1, pp. 1–34. No. 2. pp. 216–234.)   8*vo.*, Paris, 1894

———————— Documents Génois concernant l'Histoire de Chypre.
id. ib., pp. 170-6

SATHAS, C.   Vie des Saints allemands de l'église de Chypre.
(Archives de l'Orient Latin, II. Documents, pp. 405–426.)
Royal 8*vo.*, Paris, 1884

ROPA, TH. M.D. Ποιημάτια.   Larnaca, 1879 and 12*mo.*, Nicosia, 1884

BUSTON, FLORIO   Chronique de l'île de Chypre, publiée par M. René de Mas Latrie.
(Extrait des mélanges historiques, t. v.) *4to.* Paris, 1884

VIROHOW, RUD.   Über alte Schädel von Assos und Cypern.
4to., Berlin, 1884

CONZE, Z.   Siegelring aus Cypern.
(Abdruck aus der Archäologischen Zeitung, xlii., 165.) 4to., Berlin, 1884

BIDDULPH, JOHN   On the Wild Sheep of Cyprus.
(Proc. Zool. Soc. London, lviii., 593–96.) 3*vo.*, London, 1884

PADULA ANTONIO   Marie de Lusignan et la Maison Royale de Chypre, de Jerusalem, et d'Arménie. Notices historiques.
8*vo.*, Genoa, 1884

BEZOLD, C.   Fund auf Cypern.
(Zeitschrift für Keilschriftforschung, ii., 191.) 8*vo.*, Leipzig, 1885

PERROT, G. and **CHIPIEZ, C.** Histoire de l'Art dans l'Antiquité. (Vol. iii., Phénicie-Chypre.) *Royal 8vo.*, Paris, 1885

———————————— History of Art in Phoenicia. (Translated by W, Armstrong.) *Royal 8vo.*, London, 1885

ANON. Ordre de Mélusine. Chevalerie d'honneur de S. A. Marie de Lusignan, Princesse de Chypre, de Jérusalem et d'Arménie. Statuts.
8vo., Paris, 1885

NAUE, JUL. Die prähistorischen Schwerter. pp. 24.
8vo., München, 1885

———————————— Über die Bronzezeit in Cypern. (Corr. Bl. d. deutsch. Ges. für Anthrop., pp. 123–127.) *4to.*, Braunschweig, 1888

———————————— Une plaque en or mycénienne découverte à Chypre. (Rev. Arch. xxxi., 333.) *8vo.*, Paris, 1897

HOLWERDA, A. E. J. Die alten Kyprier in Kunst und Cultus.
Leiden, 1885

FRANCOUDI, E. N. Ἐγχειρίδιον χωρογραφίας καὶ γενικῆς ἱστορίας τῆς Κύπρου. *12mo., Part I.*, Alexandria, 1885
Part II., Alexandria, 1886

ANON. Cyprus Guide and Directory *12mo.*, Limassol, 1885

JOHNSTONE, H. M. LIEUT., R.E. The Birth of Cyprus. (In the Cyprus Guide and Directory, pp. 3–7, 1885.)

DONNE, D. A. MAJOR Records of the Ottoman conquest of Cyprus. (In the Cyprus Guide and Directory, pp. 9–60, 1885.)

WILLIAMSON, H. The Ottoman Press Law as applied to the Cyprus Herald. *4to* Limassol, 1885

RÖHRICHT, REINHOLD Zusätze und Verbesserungen zu *Du Cange*, Les familles d'outre-mer. *4to.*, Berlin, 1885

HAKE, G. G. Cyprus since the British Occupation. (Journal of the Society of Arts, no. 1750, vol. xxxiv.) *8vo.*, London, 1886

CONSTANTINIDES, G. M. Τοπογραφία τῆς νήσου Κύπρου. Πρὸς χρῆσιν τῶν δημοτικῶν σχολείων.
16mo., Athens 1886, and Nicosia, 1893

———————————— Γραμματικὴ τῆς Ἑλληνικῆς Γλώσσης.
8vo., Larnaca, 1889

CHICCO, CAV. ENRICO Il vino di Cipro. (Bolletino Consolare, Vol. xxii., Fasc. iii.) *8vo.*, Rome, 1886

———————————— La terra d'ombra nell' isola di Cipro. (*id. ib.*)

HERZSOHN, J. J. H. P. Der Ueberfall Alexandriens durch Peter I. König von Jerusalem und Cypern. *8vo.*, Bonn, 1886

DUEMMLER, FERD. Aelteste Nekropolen auf Cypern. (Mitth. d. Arch. Inst, vi.) *8vo.*, Athens, 1886

———————————— Bemerkungen zum ältesten Kunsthandwerk auf Griechischen Boden, ii., der Kyprische geometrische Stil.
8vo., Halle, 1888

CATALOGUE Des objets antiques trouvés à Arsinoe à Chypre, sculptures, poteries, terres cuites, bijoux. Vente à l'Hôtel Drouot.
pp. 39. 8*vo.*, Paris, 1887

MARQUAND, ALLAN A Silver Patera from Kourion. (Am. J. of Arch., Vol. III., nos. 3 and 4.) 8*vo.*, Boston, 1888

———————————— An Archaic Patera from Kourion. (Am. J. of Arch., Vol. IV., no. 2, p. 169.) 8*vo.*, Boston, 1888

———————————— A Phoenician Bowl in the Metropolitan Museum. (Am. J. of Arch., Vol. VII., nos. 1, 2, p. 19.) 8*vo.*, Boston, 1891

REINACH, SAL. Apollon Opaou à Chypre. (Revue des Etudes Grecques, II., p. 226-233.– 8*vo.*, Paris, 1889

———————— ———————— Chroniques d'Orient. (Fouilles et découvertes à Chypre depuis l'occupation anglaise.) *Royal 8vo.*, Paris, 1891

HOGARTH, D. G. Devia Cypria. Notes of an Archæological Journey in Cyprus in 1888 *Royal 8vo.*, London, 1889

HANN, J. Klima von Cypern.
(Meteorol. Zeitschrift. pp. 427-433 *Royal 8vo.*, Berlin, 1889

CHAMBERLAINE, T. J. Découverte des tombeaux d'un Prince de Lusignan et du Maréchal Adam d'Antioche.
(Avec note du Comte de Mas Latrie. Revue illustrée de la Terre Sainte.) 8*vo.*, Paris, 1889

BIDDULPH, LIEUT.-GEN. SIR R. Cyprus.
(Pr. R.G.S. Dec., 1889.) 8*vo.*, London, 1889

———————————— Cyprus.
(Mediterranean Naturalist, vol. i.) 4*to.*, Malta, 1891

FRANCOUDI, G. S. Κύπρις 8*vo.*, Athens, 1890

MÜLLER, HANS Der Longebardenkrieg auf Cypern 1229-1233. Mit besonderer Berücksichtigung der Gestes des Chiprois des Phelippe de de Novaire. 8*vo.*, Halle, 1890

POSSOT, DENIS Le Voyage de la Terre Sainte (1532), ed. Ch. Schefer.
Royal 8vo., Paris, 1890

MUNRO, J. A. R. AND TUBBS, H. A. Excavations in Cyprus in 1889. Polis tis Chrysochou, Limniti.
(Journal of Hellenic Studies, vol. xi., no. 1.) *Royal 8vo.*, London, 1890

———————————————— ———————— Excavations in Cyprus, 1890.
Salamis. (J. H. S. xii., no. 1.) *Royal 8vo.*, London, 1891

MUNRO, J. A. R. Excavations in Cyprus. Third Season's work. Polis tis Chrysochou. (J. H. S. xii., no. 2.) *Royal 8vo.*, London, 1891

OBERHUMMER, PROF. EUGEN Aus Cypern. Tagebuchblätter und Studien. *Part I.* 8*vo.*, Berlin, 1890. *Part II.*, 1892

———————————————— Die Insel Cypern. Eine geographische Skizze.
(Jahresbericht der Geogr. Ges. in München, Heft 13, 1890.)
8*vo.*, Munich, 1891

OBERHUMMER, PROF. EUGEN Studien zur alten Geographie von
Kypros. *8vo.*, Munich, 1891

———————————————— Der Berg des heiligen Kreuzes auf
Cypern. (Ausland, nr. 23–26.) *4to.*, Stuttgart, 1892

————————————————— Bericht über Geographie von Griechenland. iii. Teil. Kypros. *8vo.*, Berlin, 1893

CASTILLON SAINT-VICTOR, VICOMTE E. DE Les Fouilles de
Curium.
(Extrait des *Missions Scientifiques.* tome xvii.) *8vo.*, Paris, 1891

MAZZA, CONTE AVV. FR. L' lsola di Cipro.
(Boll. del Min. degli Affari Esteri, vol. ii.) *8vo.*, Rome, 1891

CARAGEORGIADES, J. G. Cyprus Fever, or Febris complicata in
Cyprus. *8vo.*, Limassol, 1891

———————————————— Κύπρος Δούλη. Ποίημα Ἐπικὸν.
8vo., Nicosia, 1895

CYPRUS EXPLORATION FUND. Report of the Committee.
8vo., London, 1891

AMADI, FRNCOIS Chronique de (A. D. 1190–1438) publiée par M.
René de Mas Latrie. *4to.*, Paris, 1891

EDINBURGH REVIEW, No. 354, April, 1891, art. 6, Cyprus. No. 374
October, 1895, art. 8, Mediæval Cyprus. *8vo.*, London, 1891–95

KYRIAKIDES, A. A Greek-English Dictionary, with an appendix of
Cypriote words. *8vo.*, Nicosia, 1892

DUCHESNE, ABBE LOIS Saint Barnabé. (Mélanges G. B. de Rossi,
publiés par l'Ecole française de Rome.) *8vo.*, Rome and Paris, 1892

BERGEAT, ALFRED Zur Geologie der massigen Gesteine der Insel
Cypern. (Tschermak's Mineral und Petrogr. Mitth. XII., 4.)
8vo., Vienna, 1892

CENTELLI, ATT. Caterina Cornaro e il suo regno.
8vo., Venice, 1893

MERRIAM, A. C. Cypriot Heads in the Metropolitan Museum, New
York. (American Journal of Archæology, IX. 2, p. 184.)
8vo., Princeton, 1894

ALBUM MISSIONIS SANCTÆ TERRÆ. Pars I., Judæa et Galilæa.
Part II., Syria. Cyprus, Ægyptus. *4to.*, Milan, 1893

STRAMBALDI, DIOMEDE La Chronique de (1099–1458) publiée par
M. René de Mas Latrie. *4to.*, Paris, 1893

SATHAS, C. Cipro nel Medio Evo. La Chronique de Strambaldi.
publiée par M. René de Mas Latrie. (Nuovo Archivio Veneto, 1893,
t. VI., pp. 481–488.) *8vo.*, Venice, 1893

FAROCHON, P. A. Chypre et Lépante, pp. 320.
8vo., Paris, 1894

MERRIAM, A. C. Geryon in Cyprus, pp. 14. (Classical Studies in honour
of H. Drisler.) *8vo.*, New York, 1894

MITROVIC', PROF. B.   Cipro nella storia medioevale del commercio
levantino.   8vo., Triest, 1894

CAPITANOVICI, G. J.   Die Eroberung von Alexandria durch Peter von
Lusignan, König von Cypern, 1365.   8vo., Berlin, 1894

LEWIS, E. A. M.   A Lady's Impressions of Cyprus in 1893.
                                                Post 8vo., London, 1894

DESCHAMPS, ÉMILE   La Féte de Vénus à Chypre.   (Nouvelle Revue.
T. XC., 1 Sept., 1894.)   8ro., Paris, 1894

——————————————— Les menhirs percés de l'ile de Chypre.   (Nature,
29 Déc., 1894.)   8vo., Paris, 1894

——————————————— Quinze mois dans l'ile de Chypre.   (Tour du
Monde)   Paris, 1897

——————————————— Au Pays d'Aphrodite, Chypre.   Carnet d'un
Voyageur.   16mo., Paris, 1898

DE CARA, P. CESARE   Gli Hethei-Pelasgi nelle Isole dell' Egeo, Cipro.
(Two papers in La Civilta Cattolica, Serie XVI., Vol. I., Gennajo e
Febbrajo, 1895.)   8vo., Roma, 1895

QIBRIS TARIKHI   (Levqosha, 1312.)   16mo., Nicosia, 1895

GATTO, ANG.   Narrazione del terribile assedio e della presa di Famagosta dell' anno 1571   (Published from an M.S. by Policarpo Catizzani,
Sac.) pp. 130.   8vo., Orvieto, 1895

——————————— Διήγησις τῆς τρομερᾶς πολιορκίας καὶ ἀλώσεως τῆς Ἀμ-
μοχώστου, κ.τ.λ., μεταφρασθεῖσα ἐκ τοῦ Ἰταλικοῦ ὑπὸ Πέτρου Α.
Δανδόλου.   8vo., Larnaca, 1897

PERRAUD, L'ABBÉ A.   Vie de S. Pierre Thomas, de l'ordre des Carmes.
(Mort à Famagouste, le 6 Janvier, 1366.)   12mo., Avignon, 1895

HAUPT, HERMAN   Eine verschollene kirchenfeindliche Streitschrift
des XV. Jahrhunderts.   (Zeitschrift für Kirchengeschichte, Band XVI.,
2, pp. 282-285.)   8vo.,   1895

GATES, ELLEN M. H.   The Treasures of Curium, and other Poems.
                                                       New York, 1895

JORGA, N.   Registre de comptes de la colonie Génoise de Famagouste.
(Revue de l'Orient Latin, 1896, pp. 99-118.)   8vo., Paris, 1896

ELY, TALFOURD   A Cyprian terra cotta (Silenus).
(Arch. Journal, LIII., 115-125.)   4to., London, 1896

MARTONI, NICOLÀ DE   Pélerinage (1395) publié par M. le Grand.
(Revue de l'Orient Latin, T. III.)   8vo., Paris, 1896

HOGARTH, D. G.   A Wandering Scholar in the Levant.   (Chapter VI.,
Cyprus.)   Post 8vo., London, 1896

PIERIDES, G. D.   A Scarab from Cyprus.   (Journal of Hellenic Studies,
XVI., pp. 272-4.)   Royal 8vo., London, 1896

WALTERS, H. B.   On some antiquities of the Mycenean age recently
acquired by the British Museum.   (J. H. S., Vol. XVII., Part I.)
                                              Royal 8vo., London, 1897

CHRISTIAN, C.   Cyprus and its possibilities.   (A Paper read before the R. Col. Institute, January 26, 1897.)   8*vo.*, London, 1897

MYRES, J. L.   Excavations in Cyprus in 1894.   (J. H. S., Vol. XVII., Part I.)   *Royal* 8*vo.*, London, 1897

———————————— and RICHTER, M. O.   A Catalogue of the Cyprus Museum.   With a Chronicle of Excavations undertaken since the British Occupation, and Introductory Notes on Cypriote Archæology.
8*vo.*, Oxford, 1899

ENLART, C.   L'Ile de Chypre.   (Bull. de la Soc. de géographie, XVIII., 179–201.)   8*vo.*, Paris, 1897

———————————— L'Art gothique et la renaissance en Chypre.
'' vols., 8*vo.*, Paris, 1899

SMIRNOV, Y. J.   Christianskiya Mozaiki Kipra.   (Vizantiiski Vremmenlik, Nos. 1 and 2.)   8*vo.*, S. Petersburg, 1897

PERDRIZET, PAUL   Lécythe attique trouvé à Chypre.
(Bull. de Corr. Hell. XII.. 417–20.)   8*vo.*, Paris, 1898

DALLA SANTA G.   Alcuni documenti per la storia della chiesa di Limisso in Cipro durante la seconda meta del Sec. XV.   (N. Archivio Veneto, XVI., P. I.)   8*vo.*, Venezia, 1898

FYLER, Col. A. G.   The Development of Cyprus, and rambles in the Island.   8*vo.*, London 1899

MURRAY, A. S.   Excavations in Cyprus, 1896.   (Journal R. I. B. A., 3rd Series, Vol. VII., No. 2.)   4*to.*, London, 1899

———————————, SMITH, A. H. and WALTERS, H. W.   Excavations in Cyprus.   *Fol.*, London, 1900

LANG, A.   Medical Superstition in Cyprus.   (Folk Lore, Vol. XI.. No. 1, pp. 120–125, March. 1900.)   8*vo.*, London, 1900.

DUCKWORTH, H. T. F.   The Church of Cyprus.
(S. P. C. K., 84 pp.) 12*mo.*, London, 1900

HACKETT, JOHN   The Church of Cyprus.   8*vo.*, London, 1900

LASCELLES, A. G.   Modes of Legislation in the British Colonies. Cyprus. (Journal of the Soc. of Comp. Legisl. N. S., 1900, No. 1, pp. 86–92.)   8*vo.* London, 1900

MIDDLETON, J. P.   Sketch of the Ottoman Land Code for Cyprus.
(*ibid*, pp. 141–150.)   8*vo.*, London, 1900

NUMISMATICS.

BORRELL, H. P.   Notice sur quelques Médailles Grecques des Rois de Chypre.   *4to.*, Paris, 1836

CAVEDONI, C.   Di alcune monete attribuite ai Rè di Cypro.   (Bulletino dell' Instituto Archeologico, p. 46.)

——————————— Giunta alle monete di Re di Cypro.   (*ibid*, p. 124.)
8vo., Roma, 1844

ROZIÉRE, DE   Numismatique des rois latins de Chypre. 1192–1489.
Fol., Paris, 1847

SAULCY, F. DE   Numismatique des Croisades.   *4to.*, Paris, 1847

LUYNES, H. DUC DE   Numismatique et Inscriptions Cypriotes.
Imp. 4to., Paris 1852

MAS LATRIE, L. COMTE DE   Notice sur les monnaies et les sceaux des Rois de Chypre.   Bibl. de l'école des Chartes 1re série, v.
8vo., Paris, 1843, 44

PIERIDES, DEM.   Inedited Copper Coin of Evagoras.
8vo. (*flysheet*), London, 1864

——————————— On the Coins of Nicocreon, one of the Kings of Cyprus.   *8vo.*, London, 1869

VOGÜÉ, COMTE M. DE   Monnaies des rois Phéniciens de Cittium.
(Revue Num. Nouv. Sér., T. XII.) *8vo.*, Paris, 1867

LANG, R. H.   Coins recovered during recent excavations in the Island of Cyprus.   Num. Chron. n.s., Vol. XI.   London, 1871

BLAU, O.   Zur Kyprischen Münzkunde.
(Num. Zeitschrift, 1878 ; v. (1872), pp. 1–24.) Wien, 1875

SALLET, A. VON   Die Münzen der griechischen Könige von Salamis in Cypern, und die denselben zugetheilten modernen Falschungen. (Zeitschrift für Numismatik, II., S., 130–137, 1875.)
8vo., Berlin, 1875

IMHOOF-BLUMER, FR.   Nachträge zu Sallet, die Münzen . . . u.s.w.   (*ib.*, III., p. 344.)   *8vo.*, Berlin, 1876

LAMBROS, P.   Monnaies inédites du Royaume de Chypre au moyen age.   (French and Greek.)   *4to.*, Athens, 1876

SCHLUMBERGER, G.   Numismatique de l'orient latin.
4to., Paris, 1878

——————————— Supplément et Index.   *4to.*, Paris, 1882

——————————— Sigillographie Byzantine . . . des Ducs et Catépans de Chypre.   (Archives de l'Orient Latin, II., pp. 436–8.)
Royal 8vo., Paris, 1884

SIX, J. P.   Du classement des séries Cypriotes.
(Revue Numismatique, 3me s., t. i., pp. 249–374.) *8vo.*, Paris, 1883

SIX, J. P.   Monnaies Grecques inédites et incertaines.
(Num. Chron. vol. viii.)   8*vo.*, London, 1888

PECZ, C.   Zur Cyprischen Münzkunde.   (Num. Zeitschrift, XVI.
pp. 301–308.)   8*vo.*, Vienna, 1884

WARREN, COL. F.   Notes on Coins found in Cyprus.
(Num. Chron. vol. xi., pp. 140–151.)   8*vo.*, London, 1891

BABELON, E. M.   Catalogue des Monnaies Grecques de la Bibliothèque
Nationale.   Les Perses Achéménides   .   Chypre et Phénicie.
(Chypre, pp. 83–122.)   8*vo.*, Paris, 1893

EPIGRAPHY AND LANGUAGE.

SWINTON, J.   Inscriptiones Citieæ (bis).
4*to.*, Oxford, 1750 and 1753

VIDÚA, KARL GRAF   Inscriptiones antiquæ in Turcico itinere collectæ.
8*vo.*, Paris, 1826

BYZANTIÓS, Ð. K.   ῾Η Βαβυλωνία ἢ ἡ κατὰ τόπους διαφθορὰ τῆς
ἑλληνικῆς γλώσσης. Κωμῳδία.   8*vo.*, Athens, 1836 and 1840

GESENIUS, W.   Scripturæ linguæque Phoeniciæ monumenta.
4*to.*, Leipzig, 1837

MOVERS, F. C.   Die Phönizier.
4 *vols.*, 8*vo.*, Bonn and Berlin, 1841–56

CORPUS INSCR. GRÆC.   (A. Boeckh, Vol., II., pp. 436–447, n. 2613
2652.)   *Fol.*, Berlin, 1843

ROEDIGER, E.   Uber drei in Cypern gefundene phönicische Inschriften'
(Hellenika, I. 2, pp. 118–121.)   4*to.*, Halle, 1846

MAS LATRIE, L.   COMTE DE   Notes d'un Voyage en Orient.
Inscriptions du moyen-âge en Chypre et à Constantinople.
8*vo.*, Paris, 1846

LE BAS, PH. and WADDINGTON, W. H.   Voyage Archéologique
en Grèce et en Asie Mineure.
3 *vols.*, 4*to.* and atlas in *folio*, Paris, 1847–88

ROSS, L. und WELCKER, F.   Inschriften von Cypern.   (Rhein.
Mus. N.F., VII., 524.)   8*vo.*, Bonn, 1850

TRUQUI, Prof. EUG.   Illustrazione di una lapide Fenicia trovata fra rovine dell' antica Chition e cenni su questa città.   8*vo*., Torino, 1852

ROTH, E. M.   Die Proklamation des Amasis an die Cyprier,
Fol., Paris, 1855

SCHMIDT, MORIZ   Der Kyprische Dialect und Enclos der Chresmologe.   (In Zeitschrift für Vergleichende Sprachwissenschaft, u.s.w., pp. 290–307 and 361–369.)   8*vo*., Berlin, 1860

MEIER, ERNST   Eine Erklärung Phönikischer Sprachdenkmale die man auf Cypern, Malta und Sicilien gefunden.   4*to*., Tübingen, 1860

HOGG, JOHN   On some Inscriptions from Cyprus.
8*vo*., London, 1862

ANON.   Περὶ φοινικικῆς ἐπιγραφῆς ἐν Κύπρῳ.   (Πανδώρα, XIV., 189–90.)
4*to*., Athens, 1863

PIERIDES, DEM.   Inscript'ons Grecques inédites de l'île de Chypre.   (Letter to M. de Vogüé.   Revue archéologique, June and July, 1866.)
8*vo*., Paris, 1866

———————   On a Digraphie Inscription found in Larnaca.
(Tr. S. B. A., vol. iv. pt. 1.)   8*vo*., London, 1875

———————   Notes on Cypriote Palæography.
(Tr. S. B. A., vol. v.. pt. 1.)   8*vo*., London, 1876

———————   Etudes de quelques Inscriptions Cypriotes.
Larnaca, 1881

———————   Notes on three Cypriote Inscriptions.
(In "The Cyprus Museum.")   4*to*., Larnaca, 1883

———————   A Bilingual Inscription : Phoenician and Cypriote.
(In "The Cyprus Museum.")   12*mo*., Nicosia, 1886

ANON.   Ἐπιγραφαὶ ἀνέκδοτοι Κύπρου.   (Νέα Πανδώρα, XVII., 328)
4*to*., Athens, 1866

MILLER, E.   Inscription inédite de Thasos, et restitution d'une inscription metrique de Chypre.   (Revue Archéologique.)   Paris, 1866

KIND, TH.   Mémoire sur le dialecte Cypriote.   (Zeitschrift für Vergl. Sprachf., XV., part 3, pp. 179–191.)   8*vo*., Berlin, 1866

BRÉAL, MICHEL   Sur le Déchiffrement des Inscriptions Cypriotes.   (Journal des Savants, Aout, Sept.)   4*to*., Paris, 1877

VOGÜÉ, Comte MELCHIOR DE   Inscriptions Phéniciennes de l'île de Chypre.   (Journal Asiatique, t. v.)   Paris, 1867

———————   Inscriptions Cypriotes inédites.
(Journal Asiatique, t. xi., no. 43.)   Paris, 1868

———————   Mélanges d'Archéologie orientale.   Recueil de Mémoires sur les Inscriptions et la numismatique Phénicienne, Cypriote, &c.   8*vo*., Paris, 1869

———————   Six Inscriptions Phéniciennes d'Idalion.   (Journal Asiatique, vii. série, t. v.)   Paris, 1875

DERENBOURG, J.   Les nouvelles Inscriptions de Chypre trouvées par M. de Vogüé.   (Journal Asiatique, t. x., p. 497.)   Paris, 1867

SCHROEDER, PAUL   Die Phönizische Sprache.
(Inschriften aus Cypern, pp. 227–232.)   *8vo.*, Halle, 1869

——————————— On a Cypriote Inscription now in the Imperial
Ottoman Museum at Constantinople.
(Tr. S. B. A., vol. vi., pt. 1.)   *8vo.*, London, 1878

HELFFERICH, ADOLF   Die Phönizische-Cyprische Lösung.
Frankfurt am Main, 1869

SMITH, GEO.   On the reading of the Cypriote Inscriptions.
(Tr. S. B. A , vol. i., p. 129.)   *8vo.*, London, 1872

LANG, R. H.   The discovery of some Cypriote Inscriptions.
(Tr. S. B. A., Vol. I., p. 116.)   *8vo.*, London, 1872

BIRCH, S.   The reading of the Cypriote Tablet of Dali, with text.
(Tr. S. B. A.. Vol. I., part II.)   *8vo.*, London, 1872

——————— On some Cypriote Antiquities discovered by Gen. di Cesnola
at Golgoi.   (Tr. S. B. A., vol. iv., pt. 1.)   *8vo.*, London, 1875

BRANDIS, JOHANNES   Versuch zur Entzifferung der Kyprischen
Schrift.   *8vo.*, Berlin, 1873
(Examined by Moriz Schmidt in the *Jenaer Literaturzeitung*
Jahr., 1874, artikel 85.)

DEECKE, W. and SIEGISMUND, JUSTUS   Die wichtigsten Kyprischen Inschriften umschrieben und erläütert.
(In Curtius' Studien, 6. vii., pp. 217–264.)   1874

THOMSEN, W.   De Kypriske Indskrifter. Kort udsigt over det philol.
hist. Samp. Vriksomhet, p. 11.   *8vo.*, Kopenhagen, 1874–6

COLONNA CECCALDI, GEO.   Nouvelles inscriptions grecques de
Chypre.   (Extrait de la Revue Archéologique.)   *8vo.*, Paris, 1874

SCHMIDT, MORIZ   Über Kyprische Inschriften.   (Monatsberichte der
K. Ak. der Wissenschaften an Berlin, 1874, S. 614–615.)
8vo., Berlin, 1874

——————————— Dis Inschrift von Idalion und das Kyprische Syl-
labar.   *8vo.*, Jena, 1874

————————————— Sammlung Kyprischer Inschriften in epichorischer
Schrift.   *Fol.*, Jena, 1876

EUTING, JULIUS   Sechs Phönikische Inschriften aus Idalion.
4to., Strassburg, 1875

———————————— Zwei bilingue Inschriften aus Tamassos.
(Sitzungber. d. Berl. Akad. d. Wiss., ix. & xxv., 1887.)
8vo., Berlin, 1887

ROTHE, AUG.   Quæstiones de Cypriorum dialecto et vetere et recentiore.
Pars I., Leipzig, 1875

MEYER, G.   Il dialetto delle cronache di Cipro di Leonzio Machera e
Giorgio Bustron.   Turin, 1875

—————— Zu den Kyprischen Inschriften.
(Neue Jahrb. f. Philologie, CXI., 755–777.)   *8vo.*, Leipzig, 1875

MEYER, G. Romanische Wörter im Kyprischen mittel-griechisch,
(In Jahrb. für rom.-u-engl. spr. u. Litteratur N. F. iii.)
8vo., Berlin, 1876

HALL, ISAAC H. The Cypriote Inscriptions of the Di Cesnola collection. (J. Am. or Soc., Vol. X.) Newhaven, *8vo.*, 1875

———————— The Cypriote Inscriptions. *8vo.*, Albany, 1875

——————— Notes on Cypriote Inscriptions.
(Tr. S. B. A., vol. vi., pt. 1.) *8vo.*, London, 1878

RODET, LÉON Sur le Déchiffrement des Inscriptions prétendues
Anariennes de l'île de Chypre. *8vo.*, Paris, 1876

AHRENS, H. L. Kyprische Inschriften. (Philol. XXXVI., p. 1–31.)
Göttingen, *8vo.*, 1876

SIEGISMUND, JUSTUS Kypr. Inschriften. (G. Curtius' Studien, IX.)
8vo., Leipzig, 1877

DEECKE, WILHELM Der Ursprung d. Kyprischen Sylbenschrift ; eine
paläographische Untersuchung. *8vo.*, Strasburg, 1877

——————— Die Griechisch-Kyprischen Inschriften in epichorischer Schrift. (Collitz, Sammlung der Dialect inschriften.)
8vo., Gottingen, 1883

——————— Neue Kyprisch-epichorische Inschriften.
(Berliner Philologisch Wochenschrift, nos. 51, 52.) *4to.*, Berlin, 1886

——————— Zu den epichorische Kyprischen Inschriften.
(Beiträge z. Kunde d. indg. Sprachen, xi., 315.) *8vo.*, *s. l.* et *a.*

——————— Nachtrag zur Lesung der epichorischen Kyprischen Inschriften. *8vo.*, Göttingen, 1881

——————— Zweiter Nachtrag zur Lesung u.s.w.
8vo., Göttingen, 1883

——————— Ἐπιγραφικά. (Seal with inscription, Athena, vii.,
p. 400.) *8vo.*, Athens, 1895

TALBOT, H. F. On the Cypriote Inscriptions.
(Tr. S. B. A., vol., v., pt. 2.) *8vo.*, London, 1877

VOIGT, I. Questionum de Titulis Cypriis particula.
(Leipziger Studien, I.) *8vo.*, Leipzig, 1878

NEUBAUER, R. Kyprische Inschriften. (Hermes, XIII., 557.)
8vo., Berlin, 1878

POTTIER, E. et BEAUDOUIN, M. Inscriptions Cypriotes. (Acad.
des Inscr. et B. L. Comptes-rendus, 1878, p. 194. Bulletin de corr.
hellénique, Juin, 1879.) *4to.*, Paris, 1879

WRIGHT, W. On the Phoenician Inscription discovered by Mr. Cobham
at Larnaca. (Tr. S. B. A., Jany., pp. 48–50. March, p. 71. May,
pp. 102–104, 1881.) *8vo.*, London, 1881

WRIGHT, W. Two bilingual inscriptions. Phoenician and Cypriote.
(Tr. S. B. A. ,Dec. 7, 1886.) 8*vo.*, London, 1886

———————— Phoenician and Cypriote Inscriptions.
(Tr. S. B. A., Dec., 1886 and February, 1887.) 8*vo.*, London, 1887

CORPUS Inscriptionum Semiticarum.
(Part II., pp. 35 *sqq.*, Inscriptiones Phoeniciæ in insula Cypri repertæ.)
4*to.*, Paris, 1881

RENAN, E. Inscriptions Phéniciennes trouvées à Larnaca. (Rev. Arch.
N.S., XLI., p. 29.) 8*vo.*, Paris, 1881

LÖWY, A. Phoenician Inscription discovered in Cyprus.
(Tr. S. B. A., pp. 60-61, 1881.) 8*vo.*, London, 1881

NEWTON, C. T. The collection of ancient Greek Inscriptions of the
British Museum. (Part II., ch. vi.) *Fol.*, Oxford, 1883

VOIGT, H. · Anzeige. 8*vo.*, Leipzig, 1883

———————— Ueber einige neugefundene Kyprische Inschriften.
8*vo.*, Leipzig, 1884

BEAUDOUIN, M. Etude du Dialecte Cypriote. 8*vo.*, Paris, 1884

KRUMBACHER, KARL Ein irrationaler Spirant in Griechischen.
8*vo.*. Munich, 1886

SAYCE, A. H. New Kypriote Inscriptions.
(Tr. S. B. A., Nov. 2, 1886.) 8*vo.*. London, 1886

BERGER, PH. Mémoire sur deux nouvelles inscriptions phéniciennes de
l'isle de Chypre. (Comptes rendus de l'Académie des Inscr. et B. L.,
p. 187.) 4*to.*, Paris, 1887

———————— Mémoire sur une inscription Phénicienne de Larnaka.
(Acad. des Inscr. et B. L., Nov. 17 et Déc. 16, 1883.)
4*to.*, Paris, 1887

BENNETT, C. E. On the sounds and inflections of the Cyprian Dialect.
(Nebraska University Studies 1, 2.) 1887

———————— The Arcado-Cyprian Dialect.
(Classical Review, vol. iii., pp. 48-52.) 8*vo.*, London, 1889

SMITH, H. W. The Arcado-Cyprian Dialect.
(Tr. Amer. Philol. Ass., vol. xviii.) Boston, 1887

OBERHUMMER, EUGEN Griechische Inschriften aus Cypern.
(Sitzungsberichte d. K. bayer. Acad. der Wissenschaften, 5 Mai, 1888.)
8*vo.*, Munich, 1889

HOFFMANN, OTTO Neue Lesungsvorschläge zu den Kyprischen
Inschriften.
(Beitrage z. Kunde d. indogerman Sprachen, xiv., 266-98.) 8*vo.*, 1889

———————— Die Kyprischen Glossen als Quelle des Kyprischen
Dialektes. (*id.* xvi., 44-100.) 8*vo.*, 1889

———————— Zum eleischen, arkadischen und Kyprischen
Dialecte. 8*vo.*, Leipzig, 1890

HOFFMANN, OTTO Die Griechische Dialekte. I Bd. Der Sudachäische Dialekt. (Cyprus Inscriptions, pp. 35–75, 104–106. Grammar, 129–326.)
8vo., Göttingen, 1891

MEISTER, R. Zum eleischen, arkadischen, und Kyprischen Dialecte.
8vo., Leipzig, 1890

——————— Zu Kyprischen Inschriften. (Berichten der K. Sächs. Ges. der Wissenchaften.) *8vo.*, 1894

——————— Zu den Regeln der Kyprischen Silbenschrift. (Indogerm. Forschungen, IV., pp. 175–186.) *8vo.*

MAS LATRIE, L. DE Inscription française trouvée dans l'ile de Chypre. (Bibl. de l'Ecole des Chartes, t. LIV., p. 791.) *8vo.*, Paris, 1893

MENARDOS, SIMOS Φωνητικὴ τῆς διαλέκτου τῶν σημερινῶν Κυπρίων. ('Aθηνᾶ, 1894, t. VI., pp. 145–173 and 462–468.) *8vo.*, Athens, 1894

——————————— Ἡ γενικὴ κατὰ Κυπρίους. (Athena, Vol. VIII., pp. 435–450.) *8vo.*, Athens, 1897

CHAMBERLAYNE, T. J. Lacrimæ Nicossienses, Recueil d'inscriptions funéraires......suivi d'un Armorial Cypriote et d'une description topographique et archéologique de la ville de Nicosie.
Vol., I., *4to.*, Paris, 1894

BEAUDOUIN, M. and POTTIER, E. Inscriptions Cypriotes. (Bull. Corr. Hell., Vol. III., 347–52.) *8vo.*, Paris and Athens, 1897

LOUKA, G. Λεξιλόγιον τῆς λαλουμένης γλώσσης τῶν Κυπρίων.
8vo., Limassol, 1898

CONSULAR REPORTS, CYPRUS.

Year under Review.	Writer.	Date of Publication.	
1856	Consul Campbell	1857	page 396
1859–60	C. Campbell	1862	p. 352 *abstract:* p. 473
1862	V. C. White	1863	p. 459
1863	V. C. White	1864	p. 436
1864	C. Colnaghi	1865	p. 932
1865	V. C. Sandwith	1866	p. 82
1866	V. C. Sandwith	1867	p. 260
1868	V. C. Sandwith	1869	
1869	M. Ceccaldi	1870	pt. II. p. 312, *Tenure of* [*Land*
1869	V. C. Sandwith	1871	p. 325
1870	Ag. C. Lang	1871	p. 766
1871	C. Lang	1872	p. 808
1872	C. Lang	1872	p. 389, *Industrial* [*Classes*|
1872	C. Riddell	1873	p. 1095
1873	Ag. C. Riddell	1874	pt. IV. p. 1561
1874	Ag. C. Riddell	1875	p. 1769
1875	Ag. C. Riddell	1876	p. 1032
1876	Ag. C. Pierides	1877	pt II. p. 1016
1877	C. Watkins	1878	pt. IV. p. 1364

NEWSPAPERS.

CYPRUS, Larnaca, No. 1, Aug. 29, 1878, to No. 273, Aug. 7, 1899.

Νέον Κίτιον, Larnaca, No. 1, June 4, 1879, to No. 220, June 19, 1884.

CYPRUS TIMES, Larnaca, No. 1, May 1, 1880, to No. 84, Dec. 17 1881

'Αλήθεια, Limassol, No. 1, Dec. 24, 1880, to

CYPRUS HERALD, Limassol, No. 1, Oct. 14 1881, to No. 270 Jan. 22, 1887.

Εὐτέρπη, Larnaca, No. 1, Dec. 1, 1881, to No. 12, June 15, 1882.

Στασῖνος, Larnaca, No. 1, Jan. 1, 1882, to No. 97, Dec. 29, 1883.

Φωνὴ τῆς Κύπρου, Larnaca, No. 1, (Stasinos, 98), Jan. 13, 1884, to 229; No. 1 (230), Feb. 5, 1887, to

Σάλπιγξ, Limassol, No. 1, Jan. 25, 1884, to

HELLENIC TIMES, No. 1, March 1, 1884, to No. 10, May 10, 1884.

Χωριάτης, Larnaca, No. 1, Dec. 3, 1884, to No. 50, Nov. 16, 1885.

Ἕνωσις, Larnaca, No. 1 (Χωριάτης 51), Nov. 28, 1885, to

TIMES OF CYPRUS, Larnaca, No. 1, March 6, 1886, to No. 406 Jan. 2, 1896.

'Ο Διάβολυς, Limassol, No. 1, Jan. 18 to No. 6, April 18, 1888.

Κύπρος, Larnaca, No. 1, June 21, 1888, to No. 114, Dec. 10, 189ʋ.

OWL, Nicosia, No. 1, Sept. 1, 1888, to No. 255, March 7, 1896.

JOURNAL OF CYPRIAN STUDIES, Nicosia, No. 1 April, 1889.

Εὐαγόρας, Nicosia, No. 1, March 14, 1890, to

Τὸ Ἔθνος, Larnaca, No. 1, Aug. 87, 1891, to No. 126, Feb. 22, 1894.

SADED, Nicosia, No. 1, July 11, to No. 16, Nov. 14, 1889.

ZAMAN, Nicosia, No. 1, Dec. 25, 1891, to

Νέον Ἔθνος, Larnaca, No. 1, Sept. 20, 1893, to

QIBRIS, Nicosia, No. 1, March 6, 1893, to No. 318, Oct. 31 1898.

RAYAH, Jan. 1, 1898, to June 7, 1899.

'Εκπαίδευσις, Jan., 1898, to Jan., 1900.

Κύπριος, Nicosia, No. 1, March 12, 1900, to

CARTOGRAPHY.

CYPRUS   (0. 10 ✕ 0. 15.)   Munster, 1555

CYPRUS   Insula olim Macharia id est beata in Carpathii Sinu Maximo.
Ferandus Berteli excudit.   (0. 18 ✕ 0. 25.)   Rome, 1562

CIPRO, ISOLA DE   Antwerp, 1566

CYPRUS, ETC.   Expensis J. F. Camotii.   Venice, 1566

CYPRI INSULA   N. Bonifacio Scribenicensis.   *Fol.*, Venice, 1570

CYPRUS INSULA   Ad Signum Pyramidis.   Venice, 1570

CYPRUS   (0. 39 ✕ 0. 28.) Matt. Zündteir.   Nürnberg, 1570

CYPRUS.   Paolo Forlani.   Venice, 1750

CIPRO.   N. Nelli.   Venice, 1570

CYPRO,   Disegno de l' isola di.   Rome, 1570

CIPRO,   Insula Nobilis. (By G. F. Camotti.)   Venice, 1571

CYPRUS INSULA.   (0. 18 ✕ 0. 43.) Belle-forest.   1575

CYPRUS INSULA.   Theatrum orbis terrarum, Abr. Ortelius.
(s. l. et a. sed) Antwerp, 1570–73

CYPRUS   (Insula læta choris. blandorum et mater amorum.)
Abr. Ortelius.   Antwerp, 1584

CYPRUS INSULA.   Mercator, Gérard.   *Fol.*, 1590

CIPRÉ, ISLE DE   Raigniauld fec.   Paris? 1590?

CYPRUS ISL., ETC.   Mercator, Gérard.
Duisbourg, *fol.*, 1595 and Amsterdam, 1607

CHYPRE   4*to.*, 1620

CYPRUS   (On vellum. Amsterdam, 1620?)

CYPRUS INSULA.   Blaeuw.   *Fol.*, Amsterdam, 1635 and 1640

CYPRUS INSULA.   P. Mariette.   *Fol.*, Paris, 1651

CYPRUS.   Acamantis insula, hoggidi Cipro.   Coronelli, Isolario.
Venice, 1696

CYPRUS.   *A rough copy of a map by* Carlo Tasi, *papal georgraphea*, A. D.
1700, *sketched from a fresco in the Vatican by A. H. Bagnold, Lt.,
R.E., was published with the Cyprus Herald, May* 31, 1882.

CHYPRE.   Carte particuliére de la Syrie et de l'ile de
G. Delisle.   1726

CHYPRE   Carte de l'île de   Bellin.   4*to.*, 1764

Maps in Zamberto, Porcacchi, Rosaccio, Beauvau, Purchas, Cotovicus,
Dapper, Drummond, Pococke, Jauna, Reinhard, Ali Bey, Mas Latrie,
Gaudry, Unger und Kotschy, and Cesnola.

ADMIRALTY CHARTS.

CYPRUS. Th. Graves, Capt. R. N., 1849, No. 2074. Corrected up to 1892.

LIMASSOL,   No. 846.   Corrected up to 1878.   1   26960.

FAMAGUSTA, No. 847.   „   1880. 1   22039.

LARNACA,   No. 848.   „   1878. 1   29470.

DÉPÔT de la Marine, Paris, 1873-74.   Ile de Chypre.

LIMASSOL, No. 3243.

FAMAGUSTA, No. 3242.

LARNACA, No. 3244.

MEDITERRANEAN PILOT.   Vol. II., Chap. VII., pp. 378-396.

Third Edition, 8vo., London, 1895

All later maps are superseded by the Trigonometrical Survey of the Island of Cyprus executed under the direction of H. H. Kitchener, Capt., R.E.   Hill Shading by S. C. N. Grant, Lieut., R.E.   1 : 63360

London, 1885

A reduction of this map, 1 : 316800 was published by Stanford, London, 1886 ; and in Romaic, s. a. by A. and P. Sakellariou, Athens.

CYPRUS PARLIAMENTARY PAPERS, 1878—99.

1878.

C. 2057. ⎫
C. 2090. ⎬ Anglo-Turkish Convention.
C. 2138. ⎭

1879.

C. 2329. Correspondence.
C. 2244. Anchorages.
H. of C. 151. Troops and Sickness.
H. of C. 151 & 152. Further as to Health of Troops.
H. of C. 169. Health of Troops—Reports.
C. 2324. Complaints against the Local Government.
C. 2326. Public Works Ordinance (Forced Labour).
C. 2351. Certain Ordinances.
. 2355. Complaints—Further Correspondence.
. 2394. Estimates of Revenue and Expenditure.
. 2396. Finance
. 2398. Treatment of Prisoners at Famagusta.
C. 2425. Public Works and English Employés.
C. 2427. Forests.

1880.

C. 2542. Public Works.
C. 2543. Annual Report, 1879.
C. 2544. Famagusta Harbour.
C. 2628. Payments to the Porte.
C. 2629. Financial State of the Island.
C. 2699. List of Employés.

1881.

C. 2930. Correspondence—Affairs of Cyprus.
C. 2991. Application of surplus Revenue (Tribute).
C. 3005. Finances of Cyprus.
C. 3091. Further Correspondence.
C. 3092. Annual Report.

1882.

H. of C. 17. Mail Contract.
C. 3211. New Legislature.
C. 3383. Finances.
C. 3384. Further Correspondence.
C. 3385. Annual Report, 1881.

1883.

. 3661. Finance and Administration (Mr. Fairfield's Mission).
C. 3662. Finance.
C. 3772. Annual Report, 1882.
C. 3791. New Constitution.

1884.

C. 4120. Reduction of the Grant-in-Aid.
C. 4188. Annual Report, Jan. 1, 1883—March 31, 1884.
C. 4189. Locust Capaign of 1884.
C. 4264. Census of 1881—Report.

1885.

C. 4435. Revenue Frauds.
C. 4438. ⎱
C. 4471. ⎰ Revenue and Expenditure.
C. 4585. Revenue Frauds.

1886.

C. 4620. Locust Campaign of 1885.
C. 4694. Annual Report, 1884—5.
C. 4831. Revenue Frauds

1887.

C. 4960. Locust Campaign of 1885—6.
C. 4961. Annual Report, 1885—6.

1888.

. 5250. Locust Campaign of 1886—7.
. 5251. Annual Report, 1886—7.
C. 5523. Affairs and Finances.
C. 5565. Locust Campaign of 1887—8.

1889.

C. 5749. Annual Report, 1887—8.
C. 5812. Affairs and Finances.

1890.

C. 5980. Leprosy.
C. 6003. Affairs and Finances—Further Correspondence.
C. 6020. Locust Campaign of 1888—9.
C. 6189. Annual Report, 1888—9.

1891.

C. 6210. Postal Parcels—Convention with France.
C. 6486. Locust Campaign of 1890.
H. of C. 277. Enforced Sales of Property.

1892.

C. 6764. Report, 1889—90 and 1890—91.

1893.

C. 6903. Locust Campaigns of 1891 and 1892.
C. 7053. Report 1891—92.
C. 7149. Locust Campaign of 1893.

1894.

C. 7411. Report, 1892—93.
C. 7630. Locust Campaign of 1894.

1895.

H. of L. 55. Turkish Loan and Grant-in-aid.
C. 7876. Report, 1893—94.

1896.

C. 7945. Locust Campaign of 1895.
C. 8076. Report, 1894—95.
C. 8289. Locust Campaign of 1896.

1897.

C. 8580. Report, 1895—96.
C. 8633. Locust Campaign of 189ı.

1898.

C. 8805. Report, 1896—97.

1899.

C. 9288. Report, 1897—98.

Government Gazette (No. 1, Nov.. 5 1878 to No. 648, Dec., 22, 1899.)

CESNOLA CONTROVERSY.

BIOGRAFIA DEL GENERALE AMERICANO E. CONSOLE IN CIPRO LUIGI PALMA DI CESNOLA. 8vo., Vercelli, 1869

I CONTI PALMA DI CESNOLA E DI BORGOFRANCO. CENNI GENEALOGICI. 12mo., Pisa, 1876

REVUE ARCHÉOLOGIQUE, Dec, 1871, Oct., 1872, Jan., 1873 (G. Colonna Ceccaldi, Les découvertes de Golgos), May, 1872 (R. H. Lang, Les découvertes de Golgos).

HARPER'S NEW MONTHLY, July, 1872.

GUIDE TO THE CESNOLA COLLECTION OF ANTIQUITIES, 1875.

HARPER'S WEEKLY. Jan. 13, 1877.

HOUTSMA, E. O. "Cyprus" reviewed, pp. 22. 8vo., Groningen, 1878

REGALDI, G. Le antichità di Cipro e il Generale di Cesnola. (Nuova Antologia, XIII., pp. 248–265) 8vo., Firenze, 1879

LUIGI PALMA DI CESNOLA. (Valentuomini Italiani Contemporanei.) 48mo., Firenze, 1880

NEWTON, C. T. Essays on art and archæology. (Researches in Cyprus, pp. 303–320. 8vo., London, 1880

SCULPTURES OF THE CESNOLA COLLECTION, Metropolitan Museum of Art Handbook. No. 3, 1880.

ART AMATEUR, Aug., Sept., Oct., 1880 ; May, 1881 ; Jan. and Dec., 1883 · March, 1884.

DAS AUSLAND, Stuttgart. May 31, 1880.

NEW YORK HERALD, July 31 and Aug. 31, 1880 ; May 15, 16, 1893.

NEW YORK WORLD, Aug. 31, 1880 ; April 23, 24, 1893.

FEUARDENT, G. L. Answer to L. P. di Cesnola. New York, 1880.

NEW YORK TIMES, Aug. 5 and 6, 1880 ; May 9, 14, 1881 ; Feb. 9, 1885 ; April 17, May 5, 6, 9, 16, 1893.

EVENING POST, New York, May 13, 1882 : Jan. 26, 1884.

CYPRUS HERALD, Nos. 103, 127, 129, 139, 194. 203, 205, 206, 210, 215. Limassol, 1883-85

COOK CLARENCE. Transformations and Migrations of certain Statues in the Cesnola Collection. 8vo., New York, 1882

RIVISTA ITALO-AMERICANA, New York, March 15, 1883.

L'ECO D'ITALIANA. New York, Feb 2. 1884.

NEW YORK OBSERVER, Feb. 7, 1884.

L'HOMME, Paris, Nos. 15, 18. 21, 1884 ; 6. 1885.

FEUARDENT, G. L. versus L. P. DI CESNOLA. Testimony of the Defendant, printed for the Plaintiff. New York, 1884.

THE INDEPENDENT. New York, Oct. 23, 1884.

REPERTORIUM FÜR KUNSTWISSENSCHAFT, vii. Band, 3 Heft, 1884.

COURIER DE L'ART, Paris, Sept. 26, Nov. 28, 1884 ; July 31, Nov. 27, 1885.

IL PROGRESSO ITALO-AMERICANO, No. 287, Dec. 5, 1884.

L'ART, Paris, Jan. 1, 1885.

STILLMAN, W. J. Report on the Cesnola Collection. New York, 1885.

55

THE STUDIO, New York, Jan. 17, May 19, 1885 ; May 1, 29, 1886.
ALETHEIA, Limassol, No. 214, 1885.
SALPINX, Limassol, Nos. 50, 53 69, 1885.
THE MAIL AND EXPRESS, New York, Dec. 5, 1885.
THE ATHENÆUM, London, No. 3155, April 14, 1888.
CLASSICAL REVIEW, London, Nos. 3, 5. 6, 1888.
THE NATION, New York, Sept. 6, 13, 1888.
COLLECTOR, New York, 1893, pp. 233, 271, 286.
DAILY TRIBUNE, New York, April 24, 1893.
SUN, New York. May, 7, 23, 1893.
ROVERSI, LUIGI   L. PALMA DI CESNOLA E IL METROPOLITAN MUSEUM.
8vo., New York, 1898
DE FEIS, L.   Le antichità di Cipro ed i fratelli L. ed A. P. di Cesnola.
(Bessarione, No. 41.)   *8vo.*, Roma, 1899